ISLAND OF GRASS

ISLAND OF GRASS

· · · · · · · · · · · · · · · · · · · ·

Ellen Wohl

UNIVERSITY PRESS OF COLORADO

To my parents
Annette and Richard Wohl,
who fostered curiosity and reverence

Published by the University Press of Colorado
5589 Arapahoe Avenue, Suite 206C
Boulder, Colorado 80303

The University Press of Colorado is a proud member of
the Association of American University Presses.

The University Press of Colorado is a cooperative publishing enterprise supported,
in part, by Adams State College, Colorado State University, Fort Lewis College,
Mesa State College, Metropolitan State College of Denver, University of Colorado,
University of Northern Colorado, and Western State College of Colorado.

∞ The paper used in this publication meets the minimum requirements of the
American National Standard for Information Sciences—Permanence of Paper for
Printed Library Materials. ANSI Z39.48-1992

Library of Congress Cataloging-in-Publication Data

Wohl, Ellen E., 1962–
 Island of grass / Ellen Wohl.
   p. cm.
 Includes bibliographical references.
  ISBN 978-0-87081-963-6 (hardcover : alk. paper) 1. Prairie ecology—Colorado—
Fort Collins Region. 2. Natural history—Colorado—Fort Collins Region. 3. Cathy
Fromme Prairie (Colo.) I. Title.
 QH105.C6W64 2009
 577.4'40978868—dc22

                                                                              2009021985

Design by Daniel Pratt

18 17 16 15 14 13 12 11 10 09   10 9 8 7 6 5 4 3 2 1

All photographs were taken by author unless otherwise indicated. Illustrations on
pp. 7 and 63 by Arminta Neal.

Royalties from the sale of this book will be donated to the Colorado chapter of the
Nature Conservancy.

CONTENTS

FIGURES

FIGURES

FIGURES

ACKNOWLEDGMENTS

The details of the lives of hundreds of plant and animal species briefly described in this book come from years of research by many individual scientists. I thank them all for the passion and care that provide the rest of us with a glimpse into the fascinating communities just beyond our doorsteps. Staff of the City of Fort Collins Natural Areas Program, including Crystal Strouse, Karen Manci, and Jennifer Shanahan, generously helped me obtain basic information and answered my questions regarding the Fromme Prairie. Amy Yackel Adams helped me understand lark buntings. Darrin Pratt and two anonymous reviewers for the University Press of Colorado read the manuscript carefully and provided detailed comments that improved the scientific content and the presentation. Annette Wohl and Madeleine Lecocq helped keep the text accessible to non-scientists. And without people such as Cathy Fromme, who care enough to preserve natural areas, there would be no Fromme Prairie for me to study and describe.

ISLAND OF GRASS

INTRODUCTION

I live two streets over from the Fromme Prairie. I moved here in search of open space and a view of the mountains. I appreciate open, treeless landscapes, but the grasslands did not strike me as particularly dynamic or exciting. It came as a pleasant surprise to see prairie dogs and red-tailed hawks during my evening walks on the prairie.

I moved here in April 1997, and during the succeeding months I watched as the prairie greened into spring and then ripened into summer. Meadowlarks serenaded outside my windows in the cool mornings, and I heard the yips and howls of coyotes at sunset. I watched autumn turn the grasslands golden. During my winter walks, the

View west across the Fromme Prairie.

bald eagle that likes to perch in the cottonwood trees on the prairie's northeastern corner turned its head to follow my progress.

I watched with dismay as the undeveloped lands surrounding the prairie steadily filled with housing tracts. I felt less satisfied with my new house when I learned that the prairie dog colony on the land in my development was gassed before the houses were built. I began to read about prairie ecology and to observe more closely.

Something similar must have happened to Cathy Potter Fromme. She lived two streets over from mine, on the prairie's northern border. Hers is an older development; the houses look more settled and comfortable in the landscape. She moved to the city of Fort Collins in December 1987. In April 1991 she was elected to the city council. She made the preservation of open space one of her priorities in this rapidly growing community.

Within a month of her election, Cathy Fromme was diagnosed with an advanced case of breast cancer. She was known among her friends and colleagues for her intensity. As she endured the traditional treatments for breast cancer, she joked that although she normally put in 180 percent effort, the cancer cut her back to 150 percent.

The traditional cancer treatments failed, and Cathy Fromme traveled to New York for a bone marrow transplant. She died in Rochester at her mother's home on November 16, 1992, her husband, daughter, and son with her. She was thirty-two years old. On November 17 the Fort Collins City Council named the Fromme Prairie in her honor.

Those who knew Cathy Fromme testified to her passion and honesty. She was not afraid to disagree with colleagues and constituents, yet she retained their respect. Environmental preservation was one of many issues about which she felt strongly and for which she worked consistently. The Fromme Prairie was her backyard project, and this book honors her memory.

· · · · · · · · · · · · · · · ·

The prairies described by the first Europeans to explore central North America are largely gone. Ninety-eight percent of the tallgrass prairie has disappeared from the swath of states stretching from North Dakota, Minnesota, and Iowa down to Texas and Oklahoma. The mixed grass and shortgrass prairies of Wyoming, South Dakota, Colorado, Oklahoma, and Texas are heavily altered and fragmented. As the landscape changes, the species dependent on it vanish. Estimated numbers of black-tailed prairie dogs in Colorado dropped from 630,000 in the late nineteenth century to 44,000 today. Fifty-five grassland species were threatened and endangered in the United States at the end of the twentieth century, with another 728 species as candidates for listing. Bird species of the Great Plains suffered a sharper population decline during the 1980s—25 to 65 percent, depending on the species—than any other single group of continental species.

This landscape of interior plains first defined the vast spaces of the American West and fostered the immense bison herds and enormous cattle drives, but American culture has been marked by a lack of appreciation for the interior grasslands. The resurgence of literary fiction and nonfiction devoted to this region during the past decade suggests that a renewed appreciation is growing even as the landscape vanishes into suburban sprawl, energy development, and agricultural fields. This renewed appreciation cannot come too soon. Islands and archipelagos of grass are virtually all that remain of the once vast interior grasslands early European Americans described as a sea of grass.

This book is my contribution to the literature of place that celebrates these islands and archipelagos. Living near the Fromme Prairie, I came to realize that I do not have to travel to the vast wildernesses or national parks that still exist in the western United States in order to appreciate the workings of a rich and diverse natural environment. The small island next door brings me the same sense of wonder and delight, and because it is more readily accessible, I can easily watch the seasonal changes and the ways the plants and animals of the prairie alter from year to year.

As humans, we leave a large footprint on the land. Every organism alters its environment, but our alterations are so intense and widespread that we collectively reduce other species' ability to survive. Each of us alters one patch of ground in choosing to live on it. But if we are fortunate, we look more closely at the next patch of ground beside us. We realize the losses that unrestrained human growth can cause the natural world, and we work to restrain that growth. We look with renewed appreciation and humility at the world around us. We try to walk more softly among the islands of grass.

This book opens with an introduction to the prairies of central North America, which once covered approximately 40 percent of the continental United States, as well as portions of south-central Canada. Chapter 2 examines the importance of scale by comparing plant and animal species and disturbances on the 15,500-acre Central Plains Experimental Range with those on the 1,082 acres of the Fromme Prairie forty miles to the southwest. The remainder of the book then uses the Fromme Prairie to explore in greater detail the shortgrass prairie communities that occupy the western Great Plains. Chapter 3 begins in springtime and summarizes the intricate soil ecology of the shortgrass prairie, using native blue grama grass as a central character in the drama of spring's renewed growth. The four succeeding chapters follow the progress of spring, summer, and autumn. Each chapter focuses on a specific animal—a brownspotted grasshopper, a prairie dog, a coyote, and a red-tailed hawk, respectively—and briefly describes some of the other plants and animals sharing the prairie

Grass at the Fromme Prairie.

with the chapter's central character. My descriptions of each animal's activities come either from my own observations while on the prairie or from scientific studies. I catch only fleeting glimpses of coyotes on the Fromme Prairie, for example, so I used detailed daily observations in the dissertation of a graduate student studying coyote behavior at the nearby Maxwell Ranch.

The daily activities and life cycles of all the organisms of the Fromme Prairie together create a complex exchange of carbon and other nutrients that binds these organisms into an ecosystem and ties it to every other point on Earth. This book is not an in-depth examination of the shortgrass prairie or an exploration of the people who live on the prairie. It is rather an introduction to the millions of non-human lives that are lived out on this landscape, through a series of brief glimpses such as one might experience during walks across the prairie in various seasons.

The Fromme Prairie visually forms an island of grass surrounded by a sea of housing developments, yet the survival of the prairie as a functioning ecosystem depends on both the wider world and local decisions. Let us all walk more softly.

PART ONE

THE GREATER CONTEXT

THE SEA OF GRASS

> [T]he ocean [in the central continent] is one of grass,
> and the shores are the crests of the mountain ranges,
> and the dark pine forests of sub-Arctic regions. The great
> ocean itself does not present more infinite variety than
> does this prairie-ocean. . . . In winter, a dazzling surface
> of purest snow; in early summer, a vast expanse of grass
> and pale pink roses; in autumn too often a wild sea of
> raging fire.
>
> —CAPTAIN W. F. BUTLER*

Native grasses once sent up green shoots each spring from Alberta and Saskatchewan all the way south into Texas and the plains of Mexico. Grasses swayed in the prairie winds from the high plains of Montana east to the swampy lowlands of Illinois. Across the center of North America, 1.4 million square miles of grass supported immense herds of bison and bird migrations that darkened the skies. What

---

* W. F. Butler, "The Great Lone Land," quoted in Wallace Stegner, *Wolf Willow: A History, a Story, and a Memory of the Last Plains Frontier* (Lincoln: University of Nebraska Press, 1962), 37–38.

Americans now sometimes call the breadbasket was a province of grasses: 46,000 square miles in the state of Iowa alone, and 40 percent of the continental United States, dominated by grasses. This was the landscape the first people of European descent to reach the center of the continent described as a sea of grass. One of the earliest written descriptions of the central Great Plains comes from Edwin James of the Long Expedition, who wrote while crossing the plains east of Council Bluffs, Iowa, in May 1820:

> For a few days the weather had been fine, with cool breezes, and broken, flying clouds. The shadows of these, coursing rapidly over the plain, seemed to put the whole in motion, and we appeared to ourselves as if riding on the unquiet billows of the ocean. The surface is . . . not inaptly called rolling, and will certainly bear a comparison to the waves of an agitated sea. The distant shores and promontories of woodland, with here and there an insular grove of trees, rendered the illusion more complete.[1]

The metaphor of an inland sea of grass is so evocative that countless writers have used it since. Nineteenth-century writer Bayard Taylor described "broad swells of soil" with "long, wavelike crests."[2] Isabella Bird wrote of the shortgrass prairie of eastern Colorado as "rolling in long undulations, like the waves of a sea which had fallen asleep."[3] This metaphor works at many levels. From 100 to 80 million years ago the region now known as the Great Plains was the Cretaceous Interior Seaway, a shallow ocean with a geographic extent that coincides well with that of the historical sea of grass.

Because central North America is a landscape of grasses, it is also a spacious landscape of long views and broad skies. A person standing upright or seated on a horse has a much greater sense of the movement of clouds and winds across the grasslands than does someone in a forest. This landscape of distances impressed people of European descent differently. Those born elsewhere who visited the region as adults were as likely to be repelled as attracted. Crossing the shortgrass prairie of Wyoming and Colorado in September 1873, Englishwoman Isabella Bird saw the grassland as a landscape of absence: "The surrounding plains were endless and verdureless. The scanty grasses were long ago turned into sun-cured hay by the fierce

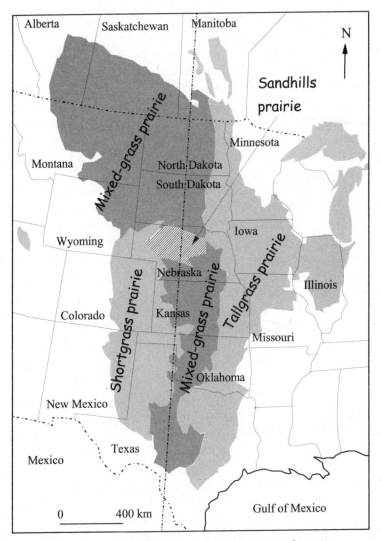

Distribution of the different types of prairie across central
North America. The 100th meridian is the dashed line
running north-south through the center of the map.

summer heats. There is neither tree nor bush, the sky is grey, the
earth buff, the air *blae* and windy, and clouds of coarse granitic dust
sweep across the prairie."[4]

Crossing the same region on a trip west from New York in 1859, Horace Greeley wrote, "[T]his is a region of sterility and thirst."[5] Edwin James wrote of the western plains that "[t]he monotony of a vast unbroken plain . . . is little less tiresome to the eye, and fatiguing to the spirit, than the dreary solitude of the ocean."[6]

Those born to the grasslands, however, became its great poets. Remembering the Saskatchewan prairie, Wallace Stegner wrote: "The drama of this landscape is in the sky, pouring with light and always moving. The earth is passive. And yet the beauty I am struck by, both as present fact and as revived memory, is a fusion: this sky would not be so spectacular without this earth to change and glow and darken under it."[7] Willa Cather remembered the Nebraska prairie of her childhood, where "the grass was the country, as the water is the sea. The red of the grass made all the great prairie the color of wine-stains, or of certain seaweeds when they are first washed up. And there was so much motion in it; the whole country seemed, somehow, to be running."[8]

Cather's sense of motion in the landscape is apparent to anyone who has seen a broad sweep of closely growing grass stalks moving beneath the wind. But the sense of motion might just as well come from the evolutionary history of the grasses that cover the subdued topography of the Great Plains. Fossil records suggest that grasses originated in Africa. These adaptable plants have made good use of the 60 million years since their first appearance. Ten thousand species of grass have spread around the world, growing on every continent but Antarctica. The grasses do so well because they thrive in the vast interiors of the great landmasses of North America, Africa, and Eurasia, where it is too dry for trees.

Vascular plants such as grasses depend on stomata, tiny openings on each leaf through which the plant exchanges oxygen and carbon dioxide with the atmosphere. But the stomata are leaky; the great majority of water that leaves the plant escapes through the stomata. Water limits plant growth for at least some portion of the time in most environments. A plant's leaf must therefore compromise between exposing the maximum photosynthetic surface to the sunlight and conserving water. Plants have enormous leaves in tropical rain forests, where water is not such a limitation but the competition for sunlight is intense. In the abundant sunshine and extremely limited water of a desert, leaves can become unrecognizable as the spines of a cactus.

Grasses' narrow leaves minimize potential water loss with fewer stomata. The blades can also be ridged or covered in tiny hairs that create a rougher surface that holds a minuscule layer of moister air beside the leaf, helping to reduce the water lost when stomata are open. Dryland grasses further minimize water losses by being partially nocturnal. The grasses keep their stomata closed during the heat of the day and manufacture sugars and other molecules needed for growth during the cooler, moister evening, when the stomata open to take in carbon dioxide. Some species also roll up the edges of their leaves during dry times to reduce water lost through the stomata.

These physiological adaptations of grasses to dry conditions can be apparent to anyone who looks closely and carefully. More subtle but equally effective adaptations lie hidden within the biochemical reactions by which grasses live. Dryland grasses evolved a different metabolic pathway than grasses of wetter regions. In the original, so-called C_3 metabolic pathway, the plant converts carbon dioxide to a sugar-phosphate compound via three "turns" of a metabolic cycle. A molecule of carbon dioxide enters the cycle at each turn and is converted into a new compound by enzymes within the plant. C_4 plants growing in drier regions use a different metabolic pathway that requires more energy from the plant but also allows the plant to take up more carbon dioxide when the stomata are open. This shorter "breathing" time reduces the amount of time water can be lost from the plant. Drought-adapted C_4 plants have a unique enzyme that only functions under relatively high temperatures in the range of 75° to 85°F. These so-called warm season grasses, such as blue grama, sand dropseed, and big and little bluestem, grow and produce seed in mid to late summer and are particularly common on the southern Great Plains. The C_3 cool season grasses, such as needle-and-thread and western wheatgrass, that are more common on the northern Great Plains produce seed early in the summer before temperatures reach their annual maximum. Survival of all species of grasses improves in stands of mixed C_3 and C_4 plants that exert their maximum demand on scarce water supplies during different phases of the growing season.

Slender wheatgrass at the Fromme Prairie.

The grasses of the Great Plains must conserve water so carefully because the combined effects of geologic history and atmospheric circulation allow very little precipitation to reach the grasslands during much of the year. What Edwin James described in 1819 as "that great Sandy Desert, which stretches eastward from the base of the Rocky Mountains"[9] to the Platte River, results from two simple facts: the dominant movement of air across the planet is from west to east, and western North America is very mountainous. To fully understand these effects, we must look back into the unimaginably long spans of geologic history.

DEEP TIME

Geologists commonly refer to the center of North America as the stable craton. The craton is the Earth's oldest geologic province and covers most of Canada and the central half of the continental United States. The region has been without mountain building, metamorphism, or volcanism—all the surface signs of the Earth's restless interior—for more than a billion years. At the foundation of the craton is the basement composed of crystalline rocks that record a more exciting time in the geologic history of what is now central North America. The basement is a mosaic of rocks created in ancient volcanic island arcs and other fragments of the Earth's crust that collided with one another to form the nucleus of what is now North America. These collisions and coalescences occurred between approximately 3 billion and 1.5 billion years ago, reaching a crescendo during the Great Plains Orogeny of 1.8 to 1.6 billion years ago. Orogeny comes from the Greek words *oros* for mountain and *geneia* meaning "forming." Geologists coined the word to describe a period of mountain building. The Great Plains Orogeny occurred when the crustal fragments joining to form North America collided with such force that they uplifted mountains where the Great Plains are today.

That was the topographic high point of Great Plains history. The low point came soon after, when a north-south rift zone from Kansas to the Great Lakes stretched and thinned the proto–North America. Between 1.2 and 1 billion years ago, the crust grew so thin that basalts erupted along a mid-continent belt. The surface remained at low elevations for millions of years as the rift zone grew inactive. Oceans flooded in to occupy the low-lying center. Beginning about 500 million years ago, shallow seas repeatedly covered North America's interior.

Subsequent episodes of mountain building shifted farther west as North America grew from the agglomeration of crustal fragments slamming into the western boundary. The Earth's surface continually moves as tectonic plates shift in different directions. Crustal plate underlying an ocean basin tends to be thinner and denser than the plate underlying a continent. When an oceanic and a continental plate collide, the oceanic plate is typically forced back into the Earth's interior in a process known as subduction. Oceanic plate has been subducted along the western boundary of North America for hundreds of millions of years. As the oceanic plate descends and starts to melt in the subterranean heat, great masses of molten rock move back toward the surface to create volcanic archipelagos like Japan and the Philippines today. The steadily moving oceanic plate carries these archipelagos along until they collide with the continental plate and are accreted onto its margin. The Great Plains have thus gotten

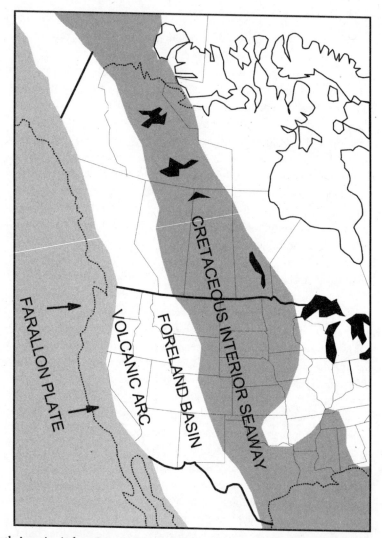

North America in late Cretaceous time, about 80 million years ago. The center of the continent, roughly where the Great Plains are today, was flooded by the Cretaceous Interior Seaway. To the west were riverine lowlands of the Foreland Basin, separated from the volcanic arc by a belt of folded rocks. The edge of the Farallon tectonic plate (lighter gray shading) was at that time the western edge of North America. Today's coastlines are indicated by the dotted lines, and contemporary boundaries of U.S. states and Canadian provinces are also indicated (after Meldahl, *Hard Road West*, figure 7.8).

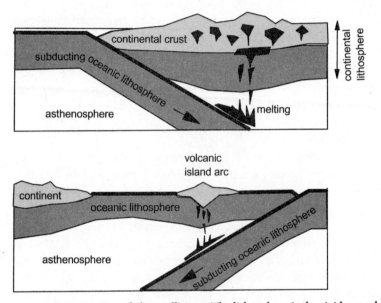

Schematic view of plate collisions. The lithosphere is the rigid outer layer of Earth and includes the crust and the upper mantle. The crust is much thinner in the ocean basins (here, dark line at top of oceanic lithosphere) than on the continents. The asthenosphere is a portion of the mantle located below the lithosphere, which is present between 60 and 100 miles below the surface. Rock in this zone is easily deformed because it is hot and under high pressure. In the upper diagram, an oceanic plate subducts beneath a continental plate. As the oceanic plate descends, it begins to melt. The molten rock is lower in density and rises through the asthenosphere and lithosphere into the crust, where it cools below the surface as igneous plutons (black shapes) or erupts above the surface in volcanic explosions. In the lower diagram, an older portion of oceanic plate, which is colder and denser, subducts beneath another oceanic plate off the coast of a continent. The molten rock rising back toward the surface creates a volcanic island arc off the coast of the continent.

further and further from the nourishing moisture of the Pacific Ocean as North America has grown westward through geologic time.

The drama of mountain building continued along both the eastern and western margins of the central plains after the Great Plains Orogeny. The eastern margin of North America collided with Europe,

Africa, and South America between 470 and 250 million years ago. The force of that collision created mountains the size of the Himalaya, which subsequently eroded to form today's Appalachians to the east of the Great Plains. Subterranean convective currents bringing heat upward from the Earth's interior shifted over time. North America separated from Europe and Africa and moved west, colliding with other plates en route. These collisions resulted in the formation west of the Great Plains of the mountainous Cordillera from Alaska south to Panama and beyond.

Wind, water, and ice can reduce the rock of mountain ranges into sediment and redistribute that sediment to adjacent lower elevations. Over millions of years, these forces spread a mantle of sediment derived from the Appalachians and the Rockies across what are now the central plains. Five hundred million years of mostly horizontal rock units record this long period of tectonic quiet in the continental interior. Sediment deposited in the interior ocean alternated through time with sediment deposited along rivers, on alluvial fans, and in coastal deltas and wetlands. Several thousand feet of layered sedimentary rocks now create a thick cover for the older basement rocks of the Great Plains.

The last of the seas receded from the North American interior by 65 million years ago, as the western boundary of the plains went through yet another upheaval. The Rocky Mountain Foreland Ranges—the eastern front of the great mountain mass known as the Rockies—rose between 75 and 45 million years ago. This episode, known as the Laramide Orogeny, resulted from the subduction of another tectonic plate beneath the edge of the North American Plate. The subducting plate pushed from the west-southwest, compressing the North American Plate and forcing its edges up into mountain ranges, just as pushing against the edge of a large carpet wrinkles that edge into folds and bulges. As the Foreland Ranges rose, water and wind carried sediment east onto the lowlands of the western plains. It can be difficult to realize this when traveling across the seemingly flat surface landscape of today's western Great Plains, but millions of years of weathering and erosion of the Foreland Ranges produced a massive wedge of sedimentary rock that thins from the source at the mountains toward the east. The thickness of sedimentary rock is reflected in ground elevations and topography; the plains are at

5,000 feet elevation at the base of the Rockies, where streams have cut canyons into the sedimentary rocks, but they drop to 1,000 feet elevation on the Missouri River. The landscape looks flat only because this 4,000-foot vertical drop occurs so gradually and over such long horizontal distances.

Uplift of the Rockies during the Laramide Orogeny created such a huge source of material that up to 20,000 feet of sediment was deposited in adjacent low-lying areas. Valleys between individual mountain ranges had filled sufficiently by approximately 38 million years ago for this sediment to be carried eastward across the Great Plains in three giant pulses of sedimentation that produced the rocks of the White River Group, the Arikaree Group, and the Ogallala Group. Each pulse of sediment overrode the deposits below and extended further east, creating layers of gravel, sand, and mud where braided rivers or migrating sand dunes left the sediment behind. Thin layers of ash among these sediments record the eruptions that rocked the lands further west as the heat source that today lies beneath Yellowstone National Park sent plumes of fine volcanic dust up into the atmosphere for the winds to carry and then drop to the east. Sometimes the ash falling from the sky killed and buried animals, as did the historical eruption at Pompeii. As a result, geologists know that rhinoceros, camels, ancestral elephants, diminutive three-toed horses, wolves, and saber-toothed cats roamed the ancient Great Plains.

The relentless movement of sediment from higher elevations toward lower elevations started to bury the Rockies, covering the lower parts of the ranges in a process that presumably would have continued until the region was nearly level if the rivers had not begun to cut downward, a process that continues today. Geologists debate exactly why the rivers began to incise 5 million years ago. One possibility is that renewed uplift of the mountains created steeper gradients and gave the rivers more erosive power. Another possibility is a change in climate to wetter and cooler conditions that produced more stream flow and more erosive power. Either way, the rivers saved the Rockies from oblivion beneath their own erosional products.

Climatic shifts occurred while the continents were colliding with one another like slow-motion bumper cars. The Great Plains have generally grown progressively cooler and drier during the past 65 million years. The retreating oceans left lands colonized first by tropical forests, which subsequently gave way to plants more tolerant of drought and cold; next by tropical evergreen trees, then seasonably deciduous trees, then shrubs, and finally broad-leaved herbaceous plants and grasses. Grasses became the dominant plants sometime after 15 million years ago, when fossil records indicate that the plains changed from partially open forests to completely open grassland. Species such as buffalo grass, which now extends from the southern tip of the Chihuahuan Desert north almost to the Canadian border, colonized the Great Plains from Mexico. Animals including the kit fox, jackrabbit, prairie dog, and coyote also apparently moved north from the Mexican plateau. Some of this evolutionary history is inadvertently reflected in the English word "coyote," which is derived from the Aztec word "coyotl."

Climatic cooling accelerated during periods of glacial advance. Continental ice sheets hundreds of feet thick covered the northeastern fifth of the Great Plains four times during the past 2 million years. The present-day course of the Missouri River approximates the southern boundary of the ice sheets from the foothills of the Rockies in northwestern Montana eastward into Nebraska and Kansas. Smaller glaciers moved down the valleys of the Rockies simultaneous with the advance of the continental ice sheets, but the Rockies were too dry to give rise to massive ice sheets like the one centered over Canada. Each summer, meltwater from the valley glaciers fed large rivers flowing eastward onto the plains.

Enormous volumes of meltwater accumulated each time a continental ice sheet retreated northward. Temporarily ponded behind ridges of sediment deposited along the margins of the retreating ice, the meltwater periodically broke through in tremendous floods that sculpted deep, broad valleys across the northern plains before flowing into the Mississippi River valley. Mammals adapted to cold inhabited the Great Plains during these glacial episodes. Ancestral elephants gave way to mastodons and mammoths, which shared the grasslands with bison, caribou, muskoxen, wolves, tiger-sized cats, and bears.

The most recent phase of glaciation reached its maximum 18,000 years ago. Archaeologists keep pushing the date for the peopling of the Americas further back in time, but the first people reached the Great Plains sometime after the peak of the last glaciation. These people were nomadic hunter-gatherers particularly adept at killing the large

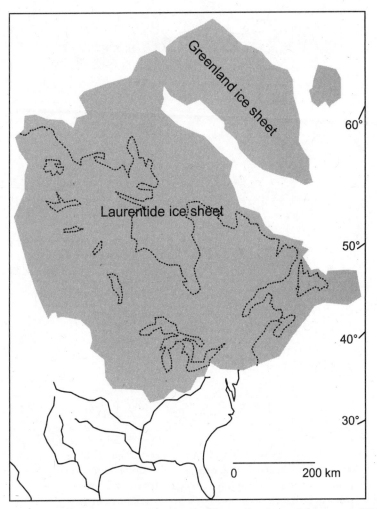

Maximum extent of the Laurentide ice sheet (gray) that covered North America 18,000 years ago, with contemporary outlines of the continent and major lakes and rivers shown as dashed lines where covered by the ice.

animals inhabiting the central plains, and these animals—mammoths, ground sloths, peccaries—began to disappear as the glaciers melted between 12,000 and 10,000 years ago. The early, Clovis people, present prior to 11,000 years ago, are so named by archaeologists for their

Extent of glaciation in the western United States at the height of the last Ice Age, 18,000 years ago. The darker gray shading along the Canadian border indicates the southern margin of the Cordilleran ice sheet that covered large sections of western Canada. The lighter gray patches indicate the locations of mountain glaciers. The asterisk indicates the location of the Fromme Prairie in Colorado.

distinctive stone projectile points capable of wounding or even killing large animals. Mammoth skeletons with these projectiles embedded in the bones, and bone beds where herds of bison stampeded over cliffs, led some scientists to hypothesize that the early big-game hunters played a greater role in the mass extinction of the big animals than did the change to a warmer, drier climate. Whatever the cause, bison became the largest grazing animals remaining on the Great Plains after the retreat of the glaciers.

A LAND OF LITTLE RAIN

Although the western plains received slightly more precipitation during periods of glacial advance, the Great Plains as a whole grew progressively drier after the Laramide Orogeny. As each successive mountainous province rose to the west—the Rockies, the ridges of the Basin and Range, the Sierras and Cascades, the Coast Ranges—air bringing moisture from the Pacific Ocean had to cross more barriers before reaching the Great Plains. The Laramide uplift of the Rocky Mountain Foreland Ranges is simply the latest crescendo in this history of raising barriers to the Pacific winds.

Every time an air mass is forced to rise higher into the atmosphere by a topographic obstacle, some of the moisture in the air cools, condenses, and falls as precipitation. Many mountains have a pronounced difference in precipitation between the wetter windward side and the drier leeward side, where the descending air carries less moisture than when it first encountered the mountains. The western plains are dry primarily because they lie in the immense rain shadow of the Rockies, which collect most of the moisture that manages to travel inland beyond the Coast Ranges.

The fact that the western Great Plains are not a true desert results mainly from the influence of air masses moving northwestward from the Gulf of Mexico. Three great air masses meet over the plains. The relative dominance of each source of air determines the weather at any point in time and space, as well as long-term regional trends of temperature and precipitation. Air comes east from the Pacific, tropical and subtropical air surges northwest from the Gulf, and cold, dry air flows down from the Arctic. Pacific air from which the moisture has already been wrung contends with Arctic air for dominance of the Great Plains during the dry months of autumn and winter. Arctic air sometimes reaches Texas or further south in a "blue norther" but is more likely to control temperatures in the northern plains. Lacking the moderating influence of an ocean, average temperatures across the plains swing from one extreme to the other in the course of a year; −40° to more than 100°F on the northern plains and 35° to greater than 100°F on the southern plains of Texas.

Average yearly precipitation increases from less than sixteen inches in the shortgrass prairie of the southwestern Great Plains through the mixed grass prairie of the central plains to forty inches in the tallgrass prairie of the eastern plains. These patterns in part reflect the relative importance of moist air from the Gulf of Mexico, which is most effective in bringing rainfall to the eastern plains.

The distance from oceans also contributes to tremendous year-to-year variability in precipitation on the Great Plains. The cold air of winter is not capable of holding as much moisture as warmer air, so the plains typically receive less than a third of their annual precipitation between October and March. Although the western Great Plains receive spring precipitation coming east from the Pacific, air from the Gulf of Mexico becomes progressively more important during summer, when it moves inland as far as the Canadian prairies. Hot, dry air from the southwestern deserts also moves into the southern plains during spring and summer, but most of the plains get approximately two-thirds of their moisture during the April to September growing season. This is what keeps the grasses alive and the cacti at bay.

The exuberance of spring on the prairie is reflected in the writing of native daughter Willa Cather, who described spring in the mixed grass prairie of Nebraska: "[S]pring itself; the throb of it, the light restlessness, the vital essence of it everywhere; in the sky, in the swift clouds, in the pale sunshine, and in the warm, high wind—rising suddenly, sinking suddenly, impulsive and playful like a big puppy that pawed you and then lay down to be petted."[10]

Much of the precipitation that falls during the growing season is forced out over the plains when tropical air surges north and collides with Pacific or even Arctic air masses moving east or south across the plains. Just as the collision of tectonic plates raises lighter continental crust up into mountains, so the collision of air masses forces the lighter, warmer tropical air to move upward. This creates precipitation as the moisture carried by the warmer air condenses. And just as mountain building is marked by violent earthquakes and volcanic eruptions, the meeting of air masses produces violent thunderstorms that fling down hail and intense rains. Describing such a storm on the plains of Kansas in mid-June 1866, Bayard Taylor wrote:

It was like a white squall on a tropic sea. . . . [A] dam gave way over our heads, and a torrent of mingled wind, rain, hail, and thunder overwhelmed us. . . . [T]he hail smote like volleys of musketry, and in less than fifteen minutes the whole plain lay four inches under water. I have never witnessed anything even approaching the violence of this storm; it was a marvel that the mules escaped with their lives. The bullets of hail were nearly as large as pigeons' eggs, and the lightning played around us like a succession of Bengal fires.[11]

Air masses most often meet in mid-continent, the birthplace of frontal thunderstorms in Colorado, Wyoming, South Dakota, Nebraska, and Kansas and the location of Tornado Alley in the southern plains from Texas and Oklahoma into western Missouri and north into Kansas. Weather records from the past few decades show that hailstorms are particularly intense in west-central Alberta and around Cheyenne, Wyoming, but nearly any spot on the plains can give rise to local storms when heat radiating from the soil in the afternoon sends the surface air rising and rotating enough to condense moisture. Even a slight topographic increase, such as the Palmer Divide that stands about a thousand feet above the surrounding plains south of Denver, Colorado, can cause moisture-bearing winds to rise sufficiently to create more frequent and intense storms.

Superimposed on these regular seasonal patterns are the irregularities occurring half a world away that can bring boom or bust to the Great Plains for years at a time. During an El Niño circulation over the equatorial Pacific Ocean, a persistent low pressure system can develop over some parts of the central plains. The low pressure is like a giant siphon, sucking moist winds inland from the Gulf of Mexico and increasing rainfall over much of the plains. Conversely, the cooling of surface temperatures in the equatorial South Pacific during a La Niña circulation pattern reduces evaporation from the ocean and allows a high pressure system to become stationary over the Great Plains. The high pressure deflects air from the Pacific northward to the boreal forest and air from the Gulf north and east to drop rain over Atlantic Canada, while the plains desiccate. Although seemingly counterintuitive, the El Niño–La Niña effects are most intense over the northern plains of the Canadian prairies and adjacent states, whereas the central and southern plains are more closely linked to circulation patterns originating in the North Pacific Ocean.

Prolonged droughts are the most stressful climatic irregularities for the plants and animals of the Great Plains. Fossils indicate that the climate has been hot and dry—with occasional fluctuations in hotter and drier versus slightly less hot and dry—for the past 10,000 years. Hot and dry reached an extreme between 8,000 and 4,000 years ago, but lake sediments indicate that even the last 4,000 years were characterized by multiyear droughts at intervals of roughly 160 years. Some of these droughts were whoppers. Lake fossils suggest a drought of greater than 70 years' duration in central Saskatchewan and one that lasted 300 years in the southern plains and southwestern deserts. A look at the relatively recent past reveals drought across some part of the Great Plains in AD 1550–1600, the 1730s, 1820s, 1860s, 1889–1894, 1933–1940, 1951–1956, 1987–1989, and 1999–present. Lake fossils from the northern plains indicate that AD 1900–2000, despite the infamous Dust Bowl of the central and southern plains, was the wettest period during the past 2,000 years. This means that people of European descent have mostly experienced relatively favorable climatic conditions on the Great Plains; we have not yet seen the worst the plains can offer.

It is in part these droughts that keep trees from encroaching on the plains. Trees can survive several years without rain if their roots reach deep into the ground to subsurface water. But if prolonged drought causes the level of underground water to drop, this dooms the trees. Because droughts are such a regular occurrence on the Great Plains, the location of the forests that bound the plains reflects the long-term patterns of precipitation.

The types of grasses growing on the plains also reflect the history of rainfall, but this reflection is complicated by the equally important influence of evaporation. The southern plains, which lie closest to the Gulf of Mexico, receive more precipitation than the northern plains. The prairies of northern Texas nonetheless have shorter, more widely spaced grasses than the prairies of southern Alberta and Saskatchewan because moisture falling on the southern plains is more readily evaporated, leaving about the same amount of water available for plant growth in both locations.

Ultimately, grasses crowd out trees wherever the amount of moisture the atmosphere can draw away from plants through evaporation is slightly greater than the precipitation. The tallgrass prairie of the eastern Great Plains receives more precipitation than evaporation, but wildfires limit the incursion of trees there. Fire is more likely to injure growth points on the branches of trees than to injure the underground growth points of grasses. Prior to settlement by people of European descent, fires probably recurred every three to ten years on the tallgrass prairie, as lightning strikes ignited the dry grasses of late summer or Native Americans set fires to improve the browse for animals they hunted. Exploring the tallgrass prairie of Illinois in 1842, William Oliver wrote: "Few sights can be grander than that of a prairie on fire during the night; the huge body of flame spread far and wide, leaping and plunging like the waves of the sea in a gale against a rocky coast, and emitting a continued roar like that of a heavy surf."[12]

Although the drama of wildfires impressed early European explorers and settlers, decades passed before ecologists fully appreciated the importance of fire in maintaining grassland communities. Fires are much less disruptive in ecosystems that store most of their biomass and nutrients belowground, as do grasslands, than in ecosystems such as forests in which a large proportion of nutrients is held aboveground where the nutrients can be consumed by fire. Nitrogen, for example, is a critical nutrient for living organisms. Nitrogen can enter an ecosystem by being deposited directly from the atmosphere or through the activities of plants and soil microbes that bind nitrogen into living tissue. Nitrogen stored in aboveground tissue of trees can be transformed to gas during a fire and lost from the ecosystem. By contrast, much of the nitrogen in grasslands is stored in grass roots and soils, so what is lost by burning the aboveground portion of plants during a fire can be replaced within one to six years.

Historians and archaeologists have demonstrated that different groups of Native Americans deliberately set fires across the entire extent of the grasslands, but people of European descent suppressed grassland fires as soon as they began to settle in an area. Fire was not deliberately reintroduced as a management tool in grassland preserves until the 1970s. Ecologists and range managers then discovered that fire can stimulate productivity of grasses and forbs and reduce incursions by woody plants. Where smaller fires burn patches of prairie in different years, the diversity of habitat available to insects, birds, and mammals increases. This last effect can be so important that several bird species of concern, including federally listed species such as Baird's sparrow, are common and abundant in prairies where fire has been used as a habitat management tool since the 1970s and are completely absent from unburned prairie. Ecologists now believe that frequent, low-intensity disturbances caused by drought, fire, and grazing by bison and other ungulates, as well as prairie dogs, are crucial to maintaining healthy prairies.

The ability to keep vital functions underground helps grasses survive drought and grazing as well as fire. Different species of grass store 60 to 80 percent of their weight belowground, where long roots spread out to draw available moisture from the soil. Grasses transfer compounds manufactured during photosynthesis from their leaves into their roots and rhizomes (underground stems) during periods of physiological stress and can live mostly belowground at reduced metabolic rates. When good times return with more water, grasses grow rapidly. The shorter the grass, the less moisture it requires to live; hence the progressive westward decline in stature of grasses from the tallgrass prairie of the eastern Great Plains to the mixed grass prairie transition, where annual precipitation averages twenty-eight inches, and the western shortgrass prairie, where annual precipitation is less than sixteen inches. Although tallgrass species are limited west of the 100th meridian, little spots of cooler, wetter conditions such as north-facing slopes or swales support islands of mixed or tall grasses in the sea of the shortgrass prairie.

THE SHRINKING SEA

Approximately 140 species of grasses adapted to the climatic challenges to become native on the Great Plains. Today they remain only as islands in a sea of cultivation, livestock grazing, and urbanization. The degree of disruption and loss varies by region. Approximately one-tenth of one percent of the original 46,000 square miles of grassland remains in Iowa, for example. Ecologists estimate that, overall, 98 percent of the tallgrass prairie has been converted to croplands or urban areas. A visitor to the region sees few areas that look like native

Grass at the Fromme Prairie.

prairie today; even sites such as the Midewin National Tallgrass Prairie are fairly small and closely surrounded by woods or croplands. At least half of the mixed grass prairie is gone; some estimates place the loss as high as 85 percent. An estimated 20 to 40 percent of the shortgrass prairie remains. The remaining fragments are larger and look more like native prairie than those further east, but these sites are altered in important ways from their historical condition. Bison are largely gone, as are wolves and grizzly bears. Fires burn less frequently. Prairie dogs are much less abundant. As a result of changes in fire and animals, many of the historical sources of disturbance, and thus variety of habitat and species, on the mixed grass and shortgrass prairie are either gone or less common.

What happened? Several things. First, people of European descent progressively drove the indigenous peoples from the plains and destroyed their bison-dependent way of life by shooting the bison nearly to extinction during the 1870s and 1880s. Europeans also hunted other plains animals from the region; grizzly bears, wolves, and elk are not animals most people now associate with the prairies, but the first historical accounts describe large numbers of these animals. Traveling along the Platte River in 1820, Edwin James wrote: "Aside from the vast herds of bison which it contains, the country along the Platte is enlivened by great numbers of deer, badgers, hares, prairie wolves, eagles, buzzards, ravens, and owls. . . . Large herds [of bison] are invariably attended by gangs of . . . wolves."[13]

One of the fundamentals of ecology is that, because of the connectedness among plants and animals that together compose an ecosystem, you cannot change just one thing. Removal of the largest native grazing animals and predators from the grasslands of North America reverberated throughout the ecosystem in ways ecologists still seek to understand.

As Europeans drove the Native Americans and large native animals from the eastern and central Great Plains and replaced them with crops, two of the three primary sources of disturbance—grazing and fire—were greatly reduced in these grasslands. The dense mat of roots created by tallgrass plants initially limited cultivation of the eastern prairies, but in 1837 John Deere invented a steel plough capable of breaking the resistant prairie sod. The new settlers discovered that the tallgrass prairie lands produced high yields when converted to crops, which helps explain the almost complete loss of historical tallgrass prairie.

Settlement of the western plains occurred later, in part because the lack of reliable rainfall made the mixed and shortgrass prairie lands more problematic for crops. Much of this settlement took place during a comparatively wet period after the Civil War. El Niño episodes were unusually strong and frequent during the period 1864–1891. People moving into the region during this time naturally mistook these conditions for normal, believing "rain follows the plow." Rain did not follow the plow, and the above-average rainfall only encouraged unsustainable expansion of dryland cropping, followed by abandonment of lands during droughts in the 1890s, 1930s, and 1950s. The development of irrigated agriculture during the period 1860–1890 allowed more sustained expansion of croplands as settlers diverted water from rivers and pumped water from underground. Progressive mining of groundwater supplies and the likelihood of less surface water as the climate grows warmer and drier, however, now make the future sustainability of irrigated agriculture equally problematic.

The new settlers to the mixed and shortgrass prairie lands also replaced native grazers such as bison with domestic cattle starting in the 1860s. Livestock numbers climbed steadily until overstocking and the extreme weather of the plains led to some spectacular die-offs, such as during the harsh winter of 1889–1890.

The drought of the 1930s is particularly important in the history of the Great Plains, not only because of the persistent images of sand dunes burying farm buildings and farmland refugees fleeing to California but also because of the resulting changes in land ownership. The federal government's 1936 Great Plains Drought Area Committee reported that approximately 24,000 crop farms, covering about 15 million acres of land, should no longer be plowed. In response to this recommendation, the 1937 Bankhead-Jones Farm Tenant Act allowed the federal government to purchase marginal cropland and put it into national grasslands administered as grazing lands by the U.S. Department of Agriculture's Soil Conservation Service. Combined with the 1934 Taylor Grazing Act, which gave the Department of the Interior authority to regulate grazing on the public domain to prevent overstocking and consequent erosion, the 1937 act greatly expanded public land ownership and oversight of land-use practices in the central and western Great Plains.

The national grasslands were transferred to the Department of Agriculture's Forest Service in 1954. Today the Forest Service administers 3.8 million acres, or about 6,000 square miles, of national grasslands. Of these, only 70,000 acres are tallgrass prairie. Shortgrass prairie covers 1.6 million acres, and the remainder is mixed grass prairie. Other, smaller prairie preserves are located within national parks in the United States and Canada, within national wildlife refuges, and on lands owned by nongovernmental organizations such as The Nature Conservancy, but these also protect only small remnants of tallgrass prairie.

While people industriously "developed" the plains, few voices rose in defense of preserving natural landscapes. The scenery of the Rockies and the Grand Canyon, and the natural curiosities of volcanic landscapes such as Yellowstone, led to their preservation in national parks starting in 1870. No one agitated for a Great Plains national park, however. Nineteenth- and early-twentieth-century chroniclers of the western plains mostly regarded the region as useless desert, a game-rich hunting preserve, prospective grazing lands or irrigated croplands, or a natural spectacle doomed to disappear beneath the advance of civilization. Thus the native tallgrass prairie did largely disappear.

THE PRAIRIES TODAY

You have to look very hard to find the tiny remnants of tallgrass prairie amid the endless fields of corn and soybeans in the eastern Great Plains of Illinois. The changes are more subtle further west, where vast tracts of largely uninhabited land remain. It can be difficult to realize the extent of alterations to mixed and shortgrass prairie when driving through the western plains on an interstate highway and seeing no other humans for hours except those in other cars on the road. Some of the grasslands stretching to the horizons on either side of the highway are no longer a good facsimile of native shortgrass prairie, however, because so many animal and plant species are entirely missing or rare and so many other, introduced species have spread and become common. Sixty million bison lived on the Great Plains prior to the Civil War. You will not see bison as you drive north through the shortgrass prairie of New Mexico, Colorado, and Wyoming along Interstate 25 today, but you will see cows. You may see prairie dog colonies, but they will be much smaller than those described by nineteenth-century travelers such as Horace Greeley, who estimated in

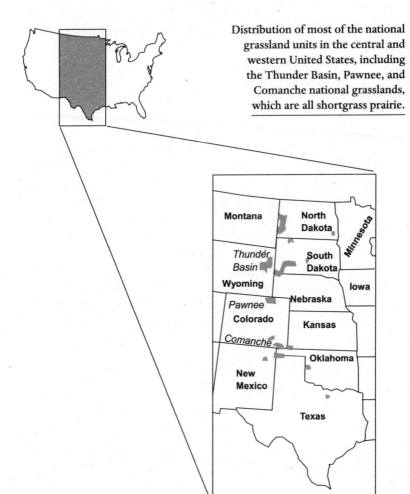

Distribution of most of the national grassland units in the central and western United States, including the Thunder Basin, Pawnee, and Comanche national grasslands, which are all shortgrass prairie.

1859 that there could "not be less than a hundred square miles of prairie dog towns within the present buffalo range."[14] Ecologists estimate that prairie dog numbers have declined by 98 percent since European settlement. Today prairie dog colonies that do exist will likely be missing the ferrets, burrowing owls, swift foxes, ferruginous hawks, and mountain plovers that used to live in and around the prairie dog towns.

Populations of grassland birds in particular have plummeted. Today, 435 species of birds breed within the United States, of which

330 breed on the Great Plains. During the last decades of the twentieth century they declined more consistently and dramatically than any other grouping of North American species as a result of habitat loss and fire suppression.

On that same hypothetical drive across the mixed and shortgrass prairie, you will see fewer grasses of native genera such as *Andropogon*, *Bouteloua*, *Buchloë*, *Chloris*, and *Paspalum*, but you will see extensive stands of introduced exotic species, particularly along the sides of highways and county roads that crisscross the land. We now regard many of these exotic species as great enemies because of the economic losses associated with plants such as tumbleweed, cheat grass, and leafy spurge.

The sparsely inhabited central and western Great Plains now present the illusion of natural grassland only to those who do not know their history or ecology. The more intensively used the land has been historically, particularly for crops, and the more interrupted the grasslands are today by roads and fire suppression, the more altered the ecosystem is from historical conditions prior to European settlement.

The native prairies present on the Great Plains for tens of thousands of years have shrunk back to scattered archipelagos and small islands of grass, within just two centuries or less of settlement by people of European descent. Some of these remaining islands, such as the Konza Prairie and Tallgrass Prairie National Preserve, both in Kansas, are large enough to provide the illusion of an eighteenth- or nineteenth-century grasslands in which the native plants and animals are still intact in numbers and diversity and the ecosystem follows its own patterns apart from human influences. Most of the remaining islands of grass, however, are such small remnants that they could not support wide-ranging animals such as bison and prairie wolves, even if these animals were present. The smallest islands provide no illusion of a native ecosystem apart from twenty-first–century humans, for the noise of airplanes and cars intrudes and structures built by people limit the horizons of the grasslands. Yet even these smallest islands of grass can provide insight into and appreciation of the workings of the rich world hidden among the grassroots, as well as wonder at the beauty of the landscape. Mari Sandoz wrote of the names given to rivers in the western plains:

[T]hese names . . . carried the song of far horizons within them, and the tremendous breadth of sky open to all the winds—winds that could sweep in great bloomings across the prairies, yellow, blue, and purple-red, or white as summer snow. . . . Millions of ducks, geese, cranes, and gleaming white swans made their annual flights over the plains so conveniently laddered by the east-flowing streams, while on the rolling prairie the great buffalo herds grazed into the cyclonic winds in their own migratory rounds, their millions moving dark as vast cloud shadows over the earth.[15]

Even a small island of grass provides some sense of the broad expanse of land and sky that belongs to the prairie, where spring comes in a flush of green grasses and blooming flowers and the little, mostly dry creeks flow high with muddy water. The steadily building heat and dryness cure the grasses to a golden color by late summer. Autumn is marked by grass stalks bending beneath full rows of seeds and the rattle of empty seedpods on yucca stalks. Thin, discontinuous bands of snow drift about the base of shrubs in winter, and the night's activities lie recorded in the tracks of rodents, rabbits, fox, and deer among the grasses. Human uses of the land have altered the ecosystem dynamics of the shortgrass prairie, but the passage of the seasons is still marked by changes in the remaining plant and animal community. These changes mirror the workings of a fully intact prairie.

I chose one small island of grass, the Fromme Prairie of northern Colorado, for the focus of this book because I live next to this prairie and can readily observe the day-to-day events on the grassland. The Fromme Prairie here represents many other fragments of shortgrass prairie remaining in the western states; these sites share the same ecosystem dynamics but also the same threats and challenges to their continued existence. By looking more closely at each island of grass, we can better appreciate the beauty, fascination, and importance of both the islands and the once present sea of grass.

ISLANDS AND ARCHIPELAGOS

*[A] land of little rain and few trees, dry summer winds
and harsh winters, a land rich in grass and sky and
surprises.*

—KATHLEEN NORRIS*

SIZE MATTERS

Ecologists Robert MacArthur and E. O. Wilson pioneered a new way
to think about the ecological effects of size when they developed the
theory of island biogeography during the 1960s. The theory predicts
the number of species that could exist on a newly created island as a
result of distance from the mainland and size of the island. "Island"
in this context does not necessarily refer to the stereotypical patch of
sand with a palm tree somewhere in the tropical Pacific; a patch of

---

* Kathleen Norris, *Dakota: A Spiritual Biography* (Boston: Houghton Mifflin,
  1993), 2.

forest surrounded by crops or a remnant of grassland bounded by a city could also be an ecological island.

MacArthur and Wilson's work was important because it gave ecologists a means to quantify how the rate of extinction (removal of species from an island) balances against the rate of immigration (introduction of species to the island). An island that is distant from the mainland limits immigration. For a true island in the ocean, newly colonizing species must be able to fly, swim, or float far enough to reach it. For an ecological island surrounded by other types of land cover, colonizing species must be able to travel through the intervening lands—fly over the city to reach the forest or swim through the dam and reservoir to the island of natural river upstream. Size of the island governs the space and food available for species that require large individual or herd territories, as well as the diversity of niches available within a habitat. A forest covering 100 square miles is more likely to include dead trees rotting on the forest floor, standing dead trees, and different ages and species of living trees—all of which provide habitat for different species of ants and termites, for example, than a forest covering only 1 square mile.

A classic example of island biogeography comes from Barro Colorado Island in Panama. Barro Colorado was once the top of a hill covered with tropical rain forest that was connected to adjacent valleys and other hills by continuous forest cover. When the Panama Canal was built, damming of the Chagres River to form Gatun Lake isolated the top of the hill by flooding the surrounding lower-lying forest. The resulting 5.4-square-mile island has been scrutinized by scientists since the lake formed in 1914. As might be expected, the larger animals trapped by the rising waters eventually died out because there was not enough land or food to support them. The remaining species reached a new balance, and the island continues to support a high level of diversity among smaller or more mobile animals such as monkeys, bats, and insects.

Scientists have repeatedly observed similar, if less dramatic, effects where changes in land use effectively create ecological islands. These observations are used to determine the minimum size of preserves necessary to protect either large-bodied, far-ranging species, such as tigers and grizzly bears, or a diverse group of species that prefer uninterrupted habitat. Some species prefer edges where two different types of habitat border one another. Other species prefer interiors created by areas of consistent, continuous habitat. The proportions of edge and interior species depend in part on the size of the island. A very large island has a smaller ratio of edge to interior than a very small island does. Edge effects can also extend beyond the actual border. A very small patch of forest bordered by cleared land, for example, may actually have no interior habitat because sunlight and wind can penetrate all the way through the small patch in a manner that restricts plants that need dense shade or still, moist air.

At the extreme, a small island of habitat can create what ecologists call a sink. A sink contains rather poor habitat for a particular species but not so bad that the species is not lured into trying to exist there. The sink cannot really support the species, however, so individuals that try to live there produce insufficient offspring to maintain a population balance. For example, a small patch of grassland closely surrounded by houses might look good to a ground-nesting western meadowlark. A male comes into the patch, establishes a territory, and is eventually joined by a mate. They nest and start to rear young, but housecats, domestic dogs, and red foxes and raccoons that live comfortably in the adjacent urban areas eat all of the young meadowlarks the nesting pair produces. The sink formed by the small grassland patch would not be able to support a population of meadowlarks without immigrants from adjacent, larger grasslands. These larger grasslands, by contrast, provide what ecologists call a source—good habitat that is stable or growing and exports individual animals or at least maintains a population balance.

The ability of an ecological island to support diverse species also depends on the nature of the adjacent lands, as well as on size and distance from a "mainland." Croplands bordering a grassland can result in invasion of exotic plants or contamination of soil and water from excess nutrients and pesticides. Urban lands bordering a grassland are more likely to result in invasions of exotic animals such as birds and mammals that can coexist with humans. Even a network of unpaved roads connecting widely spaced oil and gas wells can begin to fragment grasslands into smaller islands by creating pathways for invasive exotic plants to reach the grasslands. Each of these scenarios has played out repeatedly in the grasslands of interior North America, reducing the once continuous sea of grass to smaller islands and archipelagos. Of the tallgrass prairie, only tiny, widely separated islands remain that can support few native species of plants and animals without intensive human intervention in the form of reintroducing native plants or conducting controlled burns. The mixed grass and shortgrass prairies have fared better and include sufficiently large islands or groups of islands to support many native species without human assistance.

The shortgrass prairie once covered more than 100,000 square miles of the western Great Plains. The largest remnants of this ecosystem now lie within national grasslands in Colorado and Wyoming: Thunder Basin National Grassland in eastern Wyoming contains 560,000 acres, Comanche National Grassland in southeastern Colorado includes 435,000 acres, and Pawnee National Grassland in northeastern Colorado contains 193,000 acres. Although their relatively large size can buffer these preserves from the edge effects of smaller grasslands, historical and contemporary land uses can also effectively fragment the larger preserves. Both Comanche and Thunder Basin have active oil and gas drilling, with an estimated 12,000 wells developed in the latter by 2003. Thunder Basin has the dubious distinction of hosting the largest surface coal mine in North America, along with coal-bed methane, uranium, and bentonite mines. These disturbances likely facilitate invasion by exotic cheat grass. As of 2008, cheat grass covered 180,000 acres, or about a third of the grassland, at Thunder Basin. Portions of the Pawnee were historically planted in crops, and unpaved county roads now dissect the grassland to provide access to grazing allotments, a few remaining homesteads, oil and gas wells, and recently built windmills used to generate electricity. Both grasslands allow at least local poisoning of prairie dogs by land users.

The Pawnee National Grassland is the most intensively studied shortgrass prairie in the United States because it includes the 15,500 acres of the Central Plains Experimental Range (CPER), established in 1937 as part of the federal government's response to the 1930s Dust Bowl. Some of the earliest research on the CPER focused on livestock and plant responses to different levels of grazing intensity. Research gradually expanded to include basic grassland ecology, particularly after the CPER became one of a national network of Long-Term Ecological Research sites in 1982.

View of South Pawnee Creek winding below the base
of a low bluff, Pawnee National Grassland.

The C_4 grass blue grama, which dominates shortgrass prairie
lands across the western United States, forms about 90 percent of the
plant cover at the CPER. The remaining 10 percent is prickly pear
cactus and all of the other 340 plant species present at the site. Blue
grama evolved to tolerate grazing, drought, and fire but not plowing and cropping. Croplands abandoned more than sixty years ago
still have furrows defined by the absence of blue grama, which grows
thickly just beyond the edge of the former farm fields.

Cattle have grazed the CPER for decades, and although they
do not exactly mimic the effects of migratory bison herds, they
have apparently helped maintain the blue grama communities. Left
ungrazed, blue grama tends to form distinct bunches with bare
ground between. Grazing creates a more uniformly distributed, lawn-
like spread of the grasses. After half a century of grazing, plant cover
is 30 percent greater on grazed than on ungrazed sites. Perhaps most
important, grazed sites at the CPER have fewer introduced plant species such as cheat grass. The response of the shortgrass prairie plants
to grazing is unusual even compared to other plant communities
with a long evolutionary history of grazing.

A native of Eurasia, cheat grass now occupies thousands of
square miles of western North America. As with other invasive exotic
species, however, cheat grass has made relatively few inroads into

Short, more uniformly distributed blue grama plants resulting
from cattle grazing, Pawnee National Grassland.

many of the larger remaining parcels of shortgrass prairie. Cheat
grass forms less than 5 percent of the plants on undisturbed prairie
at the CPER. Like other exotic plants that have spread widely across
the western United States, cheat grass is a C_3 species. The C_3 exotics are plant gluttons; they succeed by taking advantage of available
nutrients as much as possible. But available nutrients are limited on
the shortgrass prairie, and much of the limited yearly rain falls during
the heat of summer, when C_3 species grow poorly. Most locations in
the western United States where cheat grass has successfully invaded
are drylands that receive rainfall primarily during the winter and
spring months. C_4 natives such as blue grama are ascetics compared
with cheat grass; they tolerate stresses such as periodic drought by
just being able to survive and reproduce under conditions of limited
resources. When times are fat, blue grama is unable to put on a burst
of growth, as can the exotics. But as long as resources remain lim-

ited and the ground is not disturbed by plowing, the natives can out-compete the exotics in this land of drought and grazing. As a result, only 22 percent of the plant species found at the CPER are exotics, with more than half growing along roadsides or in areas historically disturbed by plowing.

Roadsides are one of the weak links in the shortgrass prairie's defenses against exotic plants. Cheat grass has exploited lines of invasion along roads, rivers, and former farm fields, where exotic species are now more likely to occur than native plants. Periodic monitoring at the CPER revealed that cheat grass is becoming progressively more abundant along roads, particularly after near-record early-season rainfall in 1995 temporarily reduced the water stress that helps limit the spread of exotic species in the region. Ecologists hypothesize that the greater abundance of water along river channels and as runoff from compacted road surfaces helps the exotic species survive along rivers and roads, while the exotics can more quickly colonize the disturbed soil of former farm fields than can blue grama, which takes decades to reestablish.

By comparison, exotic plants are much more abundant on the 1,082 acres of the Fromme Prairie, which lies only forty miles southwest of the CPER. The Fromme Prairie was never plowed and planted, but it is ringed and dissected by roads, small river channels, paths, and underground pipelines and closely surrounded by urban areas in which mostly exotic plant species grow. It is obvious when walking along the path that bisects the prairie that this concrete thickly lined with weeds creates a zone of invasion for exotic plants. Exotics may also do better with the slightly higher levels of rainfall proximity to the foothills creates on the Fromme Prairie, as well as the potentially greater availability of nitrogen related to air pollution in the urban corridor adjacent to the Fromme.

Native grasses are also relatively diverse on the Fromme Prairie, which includes small areas where tallgrass species such as big blue-stem flourish. This in part reflects the diversity of soils and microclimates on the Fromme Prairie. Because the nearby foothills channel the flow of water, air, and sediment, little pockets with relatively cool, moist conditions can exist on this otherwise dry prairie.

Animal species differ between the CPER and the Fromme Prairie as a function of size and surrounding land use. Thirty-one species of

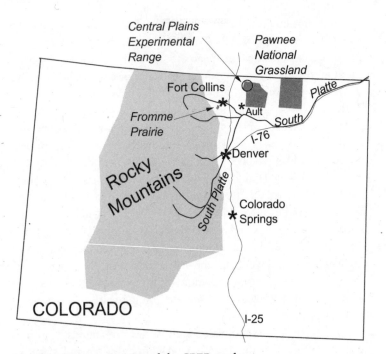

Central Plains Experimental Range

Pawnee National Grassland

Fort Collins

Platte

Fromme Prairie

*Ault

South

I-76

*Denver

Rocky Mountains

South Platte

Colorado
* Springs

COLORADO

I-25

Location of the Fromme Prairie and the CPER on the
Pawnee National Grassland in relation to other features in
Colorado. Interstate highways are indicated by thin lines,
major rivers by thicker lines, and cities by asterisks.

amphibians and reptiles occur at the CPER, compared with 7 species
on the Fromme Prairie. More than 280 bird species are present on
the CPER, compared with 99 species on the Fromme Prairie. The
particular species present at each site are as important as sheer numbers. Species less tolerant of human disturbance are more abundant
on the CPER. Ferruginous hawks, which prefer sites with at least fifty
acres of prairie dog colonies and are less tolerant of humans, are present on the Fromme Prairie from mid-October through early March,
but they are more common on the CPER. Highly tolerant red-tailed
hawks are particularly common on the Fromme Prairie.

Grassland birds whose populations are declining throughout
their breeding ranges include the mountain plover, Cassin's sparrow,
and clay-colored sparrow. All three species are present at the CPER,

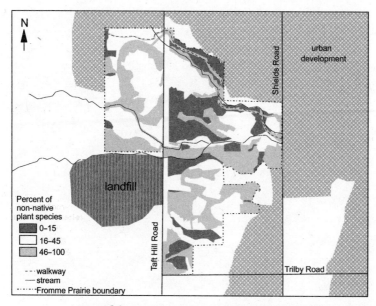

Map of the Fromme Prairie in Fort Collins, Colorado; most of the urban area lies north and east of the prairie. Estimates of plant cover composition made in 2004 by staff of the city's natural areas program.

whereas only clay-colored sparrows occur on the Fromme Prairie. Mountain plovers require short, sparse vegetation, which is better maintained by grazing and fire—two disturbances absent from the Fromme Prairie.

The lark bunting, which is Colorado's state bird, illustrates some of the complexities of understanding birds' habitat requirements. Lark buntings prefer slightly denser grassland vegetation with some of the structure created by cacti and small shrubs. The Fromme Prairie provides these conditions, yet lark buntings visit the Fromme only occasionally during their migration, whereas they nest on parts of the CPER. Individual birds can be fairly tolerant of humans; ecologist Amy Yackel Adams has described lying down and going nose-to-beak during studies of ground-nesting birds without disturbing them. Most surprising, lark buntings in eastern Colorado do better in smaller patches of grassland bordered by agricultural lands than in larger patches. The key to understanding this pattern, which is the

An upland surface covered almost entirely by blue grama, Pawnee National Grassland. Darker patches in the distance are shrubs.

opposite of what theory predicts, appears to be the role of predators. Lark buntings prefer to nest in loose aggregations of many individuals. Their nests on the ground are not concealed and thus are relatively easy for predators to find. Thirteen-lined ground squirrels, coyotes, swift foxes, badgers, striped skunks, and snakes all prey on lark buntings. Lark buntings cannot defend themselves against larger predators, but those predators are much less abundant on small prairie patches amid agricultural lands, hence the birds' greater survival. Smaller predators such as ground squirrels can be just as abundant on small islands of prairie as on larger patches, but scientists have filmed lark buntings chasing ground squirrels from their nests. The interactions between lark buntings and predators may explain why lark buntings do not nest on the Fromme Prairie, where larger predators such as foxes, skunks, and raccoons can make regular incursions from the surrounding urban areas.

One might expect rodents such as voles, mice, rats, ground squirrels, and prairie dogs to be less particular in their habitat needs, but even these animals fare better on larger, less altered ground; seventeen species are present on the CPER, compared with five species on the Fromme Prairie. Larger animals such as bobcats, swift foxes, and pronghorn antelope are common on the CPER but absent from their historical range on the Fromme Prairie. Like lark buntings, swift foxes illustrate how both the size of a shortgrass prairie and the neighborhood matter.

An adult swift fox stands only about a foot tall and three feet long, including its tail. Historically these little animals, which can run at speeds up to thirty miles an hour, lived from central Alberta south to central Texas and from eastern Colorado, Montana, and Wyoming east to western Iowa; they are animals of the mixed and shortgrass prairies. Today the swift fox occupies only 25 percent of its historical range, largely as a result of habitat loss to agriculture, and is regarded as a severely endangered species. Swift foxes do well where historical disturbances continue to operate. Scientists studying a burned area in the Comanche National Grassland, for example, found that swift foxes did more hunting in that area. They could see farther and move more easily in the burned area, while stalking cover for coyotes—a major predator of swift foxes—decreased. Swift foxes are also less tolerant of urban areas than are red foxes, which are common on the Fromme Prairie, and the slightly larger red foxes may compete with swift foxes.

Despite their contemporary differences, the human history of the CPER and that of the Fromme Prairie do not diverge until the mid-nineteenth century. It is worth exploring this history to understand how similarities and differences in land use influence the ecological communities present today in these two areas.

THE FIRST PEOPLES

Following the extinction of the large grazing animals present on the western Great Plains during the Pleistocene Epoch of 2 million to 10,000 years ago, people living in the region adapted to new food sources. The so-called Folsom culture that followed the Clovis people left evidence of their presence just north of the Fromme Prairie. These people hunted and gathered food, shifting their food-gathering strategies as the animals with which they shared the landscape

View west across the Fromme Prairie. Stalks of
blooming yucca rise above the grasses.

shifted. At the Johnson archaeological site near the CPER and the
Fromme Prairie, a bison bone bed includes Folsom stone points,
scrapers, knives, and bone needles. For 1,000 years the Folsom people
preyed on bison, antelope, wolves, coyote, foxes, rabbits, and turtles.
They were followed by the Plano people between 10,000 and 7,000
years ago, who also hunted bison and smaller animals. The Archaic
people living in the region for the next 7,000 years increasingly relied
on foraging and gathering, as evidenced by material left more than
3,000 years ago at the Spring Gulch site near the Fromme Prairie.
The Plains Woodland people who succeeded the Archaic people
between AD 100 and 1000 developed pottery and used game drives
when hunting.

All of these people appear to have moved across the landscape
in response to seasonal or longer-term shifts in climate. Populations increased on the plains during sustained periods of cooler, wet-

ter weather and then shifted into the foothills and mountains during warmer, drier periods. Similarly, we know that historical tribes moved between the plains in winter and the mountains in summer. In this sense, the indigenous peoples took advantage of shifting food resources in a manner similar to the migratory animals of the plains, an obvious strategy in a dry region with limited plant growth.

One of the hallmarks of the earliest human occupation of the shortgrass prairie is that it was sustainable. Following the initial wave of extinction of the largest grazing animals, there is no indication that prehistoric peoples or Native American tribes drove any other species out of existence. The indigenous peoples certainly altered the shortgrass prairies with their use of fire, but their low population densities and nomadic lifestyle limited their impacts at any one site.

As European American migrants started to displace Native American tribes along the eastern seaboard, a ripple effect of displaced peoples spread across the continent. Athabaskan peoples moved into the western grasslands from the Great Lakes region. These Apaches were present up to about AD 1700, when they in turn were displaced by Comanches and Utes from the west and northwest. The Comanches were Shoshones who moved down from the mountains of Wyoming onto the plains. They dominated the region around the CPER and the Fromme Prairie between about 1750 and 1820.

Members of the Lewis and Clark Expedition who split off from the group as it returned from Oregon were the first European Americans to explore the region of the prairie. They encountered nomadic Comanches living in bison-hide tepees, efficiently hunting bison from the horses whose ancestors the Comanches had acquired sometime between 1680 and 1720, after Spaniards introduced the horse to the New World. Prior to acquiring horses and moving to the plains, the Comanches lived a hard life as hunter-gatherers who subsisted mostly on nuts and wild vegetables. Their move to the plains brought them to a region rich not only with bison but also with elk, antelope, and deer. Historians estimate that in 1800 approximately 120,000 Native Americans living on the Great Plains could draw on a larder of 30 million bison. Descriptions such as that penned by Edwin James in 1820 provide some idea of the massive bison herds once roaming the plains. Following the Platte River upstream, James wrote:

[W]e saw before us, upon the broad expanse of the left margin of the river, immense herds of bison, grazing in undisturbed possession, and obscuring, with the density of their numbers, the verdant plain; to the right and left, as far as the eye was permitted to rove, the crowd seemed hardly to diminish, and it would be no exaggeration to say, that at least ten thousand here burst on our sight in the instant.[1]

European Americans found the Comanches receptive to trade goods, and reports of abundant beaver in the region soon brought trappers from the United States. The trappers established a series of trading posts at the western edge of the shortgrass prairie along the base of the mountains during the 1820s and 1830s. But it was Arapaho and Cheyenne moving in from the northeast, rather than the limited number of European Americans, who displaced the Comanches southward. John Charles Frémont described an Arapaho village along the South Platte River in 1843 as "consisting of about 160 lodges. It appeared extremely populous, with a great number of children . . . which indicated a regular supply of the means of subsistence. The chiefs . . . received us (as probably strangers are always received to whom they desire to show respect or regard) by throwing their arms around our necks and embracing us."[2]

The Arapaho and Cheyenne occupied the area around the CPER and the Fromme Prairie until about 1870. Along with the Pawnee living further east along the Colorado-Nebraska border, they bore the brunt of the endless flood of European Americans that soon began to engulf them from the east. Discoveries of gold and silver deposits near Denver in 1859 and throughout the mountains on the western borders of the shortgrass prairie during the 1860s and 1870s quickly brought thousands of people to the region. As towns sprang up around mining centers, roads and railroads split off from the main emigrant trails along the Platte River toward fur-trapping posts and up into the mountains. Other towns began to grow on the plains. Little in their culture or history had prepared the Native Americans for the sustained ferocity of the warfare that accompanied the European American migration. Isolated, unreported murders escalated into infamous massacres such as that at Sand Creek, Colorado, in 1864.

Such events swiftly changed the human face of the landscape. The European Americans largely exterminated the Arapaho, Cheyenne, and Pawnee from Colorado, leaving only a small band of Utes on a reservation in the southwestern portion of the state.

MANIFEST DESTINY?

Farmers from the United States quickly claimed the prairie lands vacated by the removal of the Native Americans. Edwin James described a Pawnee village in 1820 in which the inhabitants planted "corn and pumpkins in little patches along the sides of deep ravines, and wherever by any accident the grassy turf has been eradicated," using "rude instruments of wood and bone."[3] The Pawnee tended the first farms on the Colorado prairie, but these plantings were dwarfed by the large fields soon plowed up by the European Americans. Nathan Meeker founded an agricultural colony northeast of the Fromme Prairie and west of the CPER in 1870, diverting water from the Poudre and South Platte rivers to grow wheat. Immediately adjacent to the Fromme Prairie, a group of investors formed a company to purchase land around the abandoned military reservation of Camp Collins. Lots went up for sale in the Fort Collins Agricultural Colony in 1873, and farmers dug the town's irrigation ditch the same year.

This is the point in time at which the history of land use starts to diverge between the CPER and the Fromme Prairie. Lying closer to the mountains and foothills, the lands around the Fromme Prairie were nearer to regional transportation networks of roads and stagecoach routes and to streams fed by mountain snowmelt that could be diverted for agriculture. Urban centers grew much faster in the corridor at the eastern base of the mountains from Fort Collins south through Denver to Colorado Springs than they did on the plains even a few miles farther east around the CPER. Farmers in both the more densely settled corridor and farther east of the mountains swiftly changed the distribution of water across the shortgrass prairie.

The farmers settling the western margins of the Great Plains believed they were following their manifest destiny. They faced severe climatic constraints, however, in trying to grow crops that required a steady and relatively abundant supply of water. This dry region was on the very threshold of mobilizing sand-sized particles and turning a prairie into sand dunes. When the first farmers settled here in the 1860s, they planted their crops across low, rolling hills formed of old dunes barely stabilized by shortgrasses and shrubs. The dunes had been active periodically during the 10,000 years since the great valley glaciers had melted in the Colorado Front Range. When the climate grew a little hotter and drier and the vegetation lost ground, the dunes returned as winds from the northwest picked up sand from the broad floodplain of the South Platte River or the basins along the mountain front, distributing the sands in dune fields across eastern Colorado and into the Sandhills region of western Nebraska. Dunes spread across portions of eastern Colorado three times between 9,500 and 1,500 years ago and then episodically from 1,000 years ago up to AD 1800. In the moister periods between, vegetation stabilized the dunes and soils formed. During the thousands of years preceding European settlement of the region, nomadic hunter-gatherer peoples shifted toward the foothills during periods of dune activity and moved back onto the plains during cooler, wetter periods.

Historically, a network of dry stream channels creased the drylands of the prairie. These smaller channels flowed only briefly after snowmelt or rainfall, then shrank back to isolated pools that retained water throughout the year. Many of the small native fish of the western plains adapted to this harsh regime, using the brief period of connected flow to move about and breed and laying eggs that developed unusually fast. These fish can survive dry seasons in isolated pools because they can withstand warm water temperatures and low levels of dissolved oxygen, but the existence of the pools is crucial to their survival. The pools also provide a rare source of surface water to other animals in the drylands of the shortgrass prairie; although many native animals have evolved to obtain sufficient water from their food without drinking, some species of birds and other animals will travel long distances to drink from pools and seeps.

The presence of underground water at shallow depths is necessary to maintain water in the pools. All of the sand, silt, and gravel shed eastward during periods of sustained erosion of the ancestral Rocky Mountains created a thick wedge of sediment that can now retain subsurface water. The single greatest underground water storage is in the Ogallala Aquifer, which spreads beneath the shortgrass and western mixed grass prairies. Rainfall and snowmelt gradually

Dry stream channels, Pawnee National Grassland. The channel
above has depressions that sometimes hold water throughout the
year; in this photo the depressions are filled with tumbleweed.
The channel below contains water for only hours after rainfall.

Refuge pool, Pawnee National Grassland; photo taken in October 2008. This pool holds enough water to sustain fish throughout the winter until connected stream flow returns briefly in the spring.

infiltrating the ground over thousands of years built up this underground reserve that sustained seeps, springs, and small streams across the western plains.

Larger prairie streams that headed in the mountains flowed throughout the year, fed by the high country's gradually melting snowpack as it ran across the surface or percolated through the subsurface to emerge downslope in seeps and springs. During the spring and early summer the larger rivers flowed high and muddy with meltwater from the Rockies. As the snowpack disappeared and the cooler temperatures of autumn and winter arrived, the rivers shrank back to narrow, shallow channels bordered by broad floodplains. Trees had little chance to become established on these floodplains, for the levels of subsurface water fell during the dry season and the turbulent floods the next spring could rip out new seedlings. In the absence of stabilizing vegetation, the swift floodwaters easily eroded the stream

Map of the area in the western Great Plains underlain by the Ogallala Aquifer (gray).

banks. The streams continually shifted back and forth, creating broad, braided channels. During some years, even the largest streams were nearly dry by the time they reached the Colorado-Nebraska border.

These broad, shallow streams supported one of the continent's great pathways for migratory waterfowl. As Mari Sandoz wrote in *Love Song to the Plains*, "[M]illions of ducks, geese, cranes, and gleaming white swans made their annual flights over the plains so conveniently laddered by the east-flowing streams."[4] The river channels provided stopover sites where hungry birds ate the plant roots, invertebrates, and small animals such as amphibians that provided sufficient fuel to continue on their long flights. Thousands of birds at a time spread across the extensive sandbars and floodplains where open ground allowed them to see predators approaching.

The farmers settling the shortgrass prairie starting in the 1860s brought with them crops from the eastern and midwestern United States and the belief that "rain follows the plow." Fourteen inches of moisture, fluctuating between six inches in a dry year and twenty-seven inches in a wet year, were insufficient for most of these crops, however. Rain did not follow the plow.

Railroad bridge destroyed by a 1935 flood on the South Platte
River in Fort Morgan, Colorado, twenty-five miles south
of the Pawnee National Grassland. Note the wide, shallow
channel and the complete absence of trees and shrubs along
the stream banks. Courtesy, Colorado Historical Society.

But water could be brought to the crops from the rivers that
flowed high with melting snow through the summer. The farmers
formed irrigation companies and water conservancy districts. First
the territorial government, then the state and federal governments,
helped them alter for human uses the grasslands explorers Zebu-
lon Pike and Stephen Long called the Great American Desert. The
farmers built storage reservoirs high in the mountains, damming
the alpine lakes, and they dug other reservoirs into the flat plains.
They blasted tunnels through the mountains with dynamite and
hand tools, diverting water from the more sparsely settled western
slope of the Rockies and the Colorado River and bringing it instead
to the eastern slope and the drainage of the Platte and Missouri rivers.
From these reservoirs and tunnels the farmers spread the nourishing
waters across the dry plains in hundreds of miles of irrigation canals,
creating their own topography to get the water where they wanted
it. The prodigal spring and summer floods of the rivers were stored in
reservoirs and released slowly throughout the growing season. Much
of the water spread thickly across the farm fields evaporated, and
much of it soaked deep into the ground, raising local water tables.

Trees, no longer ripped out by floods or dessicated in autumn, began to spread from isolated patches along the riverbanks. As the trees grew, they increased the resistance of stream banks to erosion and trapped more sediment, so the stream channels narrowed. Streams that had been well over 1,000 feet wide and braided when the first European Americans arrived midway through the nineteenth century had narrowed to 300 feet and meandered among dense riverside forests by the early twentieth century. These river lines of deciduous forests formed migration corridors that drew eastern species westward. White-tailed deer invaded the range of native mule deer, and blue jays from the eastern woodlands mingled with western scrub jays. Stream waters that had been warm and turbid grew cooler and clearer, stressing native fish communities. Migrating cranes lost the wet meadows and marshlands they needed for feeding and resting during their long journeys.

Downstream view of the South Platte River in Fort Morgan, Colorado, in 2008. The river is much narrower and more densely lined with vegetation than in the 1935 view.

As the number of farmers and the demand for water increased, all available water in rivers was claimed. Further expansion of croplands and agricultural communities required pumping groundwater. Improved technology and greater demand led to increasing extraction of groundwater during the waning decades of the nineteenth century, a process that accelerated during the twentieth century. If groundwater is pumped up faster than it is naturally resupplied by infiltrating precipitation, the surface of the underground water, known as the water table, begins to drop. Initially this occurs in the immediate vicinity of each well, but eventually it can lower regional water tables. By the end of the twentieth century, approximately half of the 977 trillion gallons of groundwater stored in the Ogallala Aquifer had been removed by pumping. The water table has dropped more than 20 feet beneath approximately 1,900 square miles of eastern Colorado.

As water tables drop, seeps and springs begin to dry up. Smaller streams flow for a shorter period in the summer or cease to flow altogether. The refuge pools on which fish depend no longer retain water throughout the year, and species such as the brassy minnow slip toward extinction.

Despite all the water engineering, those farming the shortgrass prairie were unable to insure themselves against crop failure. Severe droughts in the 1930s created a Dust Bowl across the Great Plains, causing huge human population shifts as starving rural families left dust-dry farms. The dry winds lifted the thin layer of organic soil and carried it off, compromising the soil's ability to support any vegetation as the nutrient cycling of the prairie and the carbon and nitrogen storage reservoir in the soil broke down. Another severe drought in the 1950s and lesser droughts in the 1970s did not quite mobilize the sand dunes of eastern Colorado, but they adversely affected regional agriculture and produced more rounds of reservoir construction and groundwater pumping. Determined agriculturalists pushed through the Colorado–Big Thompson Project, which by 1957 diverted approximately 75 billion gallons of water from the Colorado River through Big Thompson Canyon to the South Platte River and the eastern slope of the Rockies. Today more than half of the South Platte's average yearly flow at the eastern border of Colorado comes from the other side of the Rockies.

Declining water tables did not dramatically affect the lands of the CPER or the Fromme Prairie. Much of the cropland on the CPER was taken out of production prior to the use of high-powered groundwater pumps, so local water tables did not exhibit the severe declines present elsewhere on the shortgrass prairie. The Fromme Prairie was grazed rather than plowed and lies sufficiently close to the mountain front that most water for agriculture comes from diverted stream flow rather than groundwater. But the South Platte River to the south of the CPER has undergone dramatic changes as a result of altered stream flows, as has its tributary the Poudre River that flows north of the Fromme Prairie. Both rivers have also undergone important changes in water quality as a result of land use during the twentieth century.

CHEMICAL LEGACY

Ever since the Green Revolution that followed World War II, farmers have applied massive quantities of fertilizer to the drylands to support an expanding annual monoculture of crops and equally massive applications of pesticides to keep the crops from feeding any insects that might fancy their taste.

Much of the fertilizer applied is not used by the crop plants and accumulates in the soil, surface water, and groundwater. There the nutrients can build to concentrations that effectively poison living organisms. Similarly, one of the latent tragedies of pesticides is that many of them bind to organic matter in soil, the great reservoir of carbon on which all living organisms ultimately draw. Further, soil is not the only casualty of introduced contaminants. Decades after agriculture reached the Great Plains, the U.S. government began a national inventory of surface water and groundwater quality. The South Platte River drainage was chosen as one of the sampling basins. Scientists from the U.S. Geological Survey set up nearly 300 sampling sites throughout the drainage, from mountain streams at 14,000 feet in elevation to sites in eastern Colorado and western Nebraska. At these sites the scientists analyzed groundwater and surface water chemistry, streambed sediments, stream habitat, and fish tissues. They published the first round of analyses in 1998.[5]

Forested mountain streams were generally in good condition unless pollutants from mining had dissolved in the water. But moving downstream onto the plains, into urban and agricultural lands, many streams were ecological disasters. Alteration of the natural seasonal water flow had damaged native aquatic habitat. Compounds such as polychlorinated biphenyls (PCBs) and chlordane, widely used in urban areas historically but now banned, were still detected in fish tissue. In addition to currently used pesticides, other pesticides such as dieldrin and DDT (dichlorophenyl tricholoroethane; banned since 1972) were detected in streambed sediments and fish tissue collected from urban and agricultural lands. The surface water in agricultural sites contained an alarming brew of up to twenty-five pesticides.

Groundwater can be equally contaminated in agricultural and urban areas. High nitrate concentrations leaching from crop fertilizers have so degraded groundwater quality that wells in some towns on the eastern plains of Colorado can no longer be used to supply drinking water. The U.S. Geological Survey study detected fifteen different pesticides in groundwater of the South Platte River basin. At least one type of pesticide was detected in twenty-nine of the thirty groundwater wells sampled in the agricultural portion of the basin between eastern Colorado and western Nebraska. Volatile organic compounds derived from gasoline and cleaning solvents were detected in 86 percent of shallow urban groundwater samples.

Waters on the CPER and the Fromme Prairie are fairly clean because these lands escaped the intensive, industrial-scale agriculture of the late twentieth century. Very few people live or farm in the vicinity of the CPER today. Cattle congregating at pools or springs can increase nitrogen levels in surface water, but this effect is very local.

On the Fromme Prairie, no agriculture is practiced upslope, and there are few houses to the west. But the prairie is closely encroached by humans and their toxic wastes on its other boundaries. Runoff from adjacent roads, lawns, and construction areas brings contaminants including nitrates, phosphates, cadmium, and mercury to the prairie. The amount of nitrogen and phosphorus present can change the soil microbial community and the plant species composition, altering the entire delicately balanced cycle of carbon, nitrogen, and other nutrients on the prairie. Cadmium and mercury, endocrine disrupters, block communication between cells in developing embryos. The results are far-reaching. Endocrine disruption produces changes as diverse as birds born with crossed bills and increasing rates of cancer in humans.

Immediately southwest of the Fromme Prairie lies the Larimer County Landfill. Contaminants leaching from this landfill, which is slightly upslope, have the potential to contaminate groundwater flowing toward the prairie. Contaminants can include volatile compounds such as vinyl chloride from polyvinyl chloride (pvc) and other polymers, the industrial solvents and de-greasers trichloroethene and methyl chloroform, and heavy metals such as lead from gasoline or hunting shot. From the groundwater, these contaminants make their way through the food chain. As the groundwater moves through the soil, some of the contaminants bind to clay particles. Others will be taken up by the millions of soil microorganisms and passed along to the next level of predators.

Because many of the toxins an animal ingests are stored in its tissues rather than excreted, an individual animal can accumulate toxins throughout its life and pass them along to its predators. Thus, the contaminants may pass into prairie plants, be ingested by an earthworm, pass to a shrew, and thence to a red fox. If the shrew eats enough worms and the fox eats enough shrews, the fox will carry a concentrated dose of contaminants in its body. Aquatic insects may take up some of the contaminants while ingesting the organic-rich muck at the base of a marsh. A mallard will then concentrate the insects' intake and pass the contaminants in its own tissues to a great-horned owl. From the seeds of the prairie vegetation, meadow voles will pass lethal substances on to golden eagles, and prairie dogs will store contaminants from the grass for later concentration by a red-tailed hawk. The chemical legacy of industrial farming and urbanization on adjacent lands may be largely invisible on the shortgrass prairie, but that does not diminish its importance.

The effects of human activities on the shortgrass prairie thus go far beyond removing native prairie plants to grow crops or build houses. Size and internal fragmentation of the prairie by features such as roads matter because they influence whether interior or edge species are present, how much space is available for wide-ranging species, and what types of inroads can be made by exotic invasive species. History matters because it reflects the natural (fire, grazing by bison and prairie dogs, drought) and human-induced (crops,

Looking west toward the foothills and the neighborhoods
bordering the Fromme Prairie; yucca in the foreground.

groundwater withdrawal, surface water diversion) disturbances that
influence plant and animal species on the prairie, as well as resources
available. Neighbors also matter because they influence contaminants and exotic species entering the prairie. The remaining islands
and archipelagos of shortgrass prairie in the western United States
reflect all of these influences in ways we do not yet fully understand
but that comparisons of different islands of grass, such as the CPER
and the Fromme Prairie, continue to illuminate.

PART TWO

THE FROMME PRAIRIE

GRASSROOTS

A child said "What is the grass?" fetching it to me with full hands, How could I answer the child? I do not know what it is any more than he.

—WALT WHITMAN, "SONG OF MYSELF"*

At the base of the Colorado Front Range lies a tiny patch of undulating grassland that occupies the boundary between two of the continent's enormous physiographic regions: the wide-spreading interior plains to the east and the broad band of the Rockies to the west. Geology, topography, climate, and ecological communities differ dramatically east and west of this point on Earth. Eastward there is no boundary but the distant meeting of land and sky. Westward the first row of the foothills forms a solid dark line on the western

---

* Walt Whitman, "Song of Myself," in *Leaves of Grass* (New York: Doubleday, 1940), 39.

View west, across yucca on a hill slope at the
Fromme Prairie to the forested foothills.

horizon each evening. This line marks the western limits of the
grassland. The land rises steeply into rocky slopes on which tough
mountain mahogany bushes and gnarled ponderosa pine trees start
to displace the grasses. Further west, beyond the first row of foothills, lodgepole pines and spruce and fir replace the ponderosas and
eventually give way to alpine meadows thousands of feet higher in
elevation than the prairie.

At the base of the foothills, flat-topped old stream terraces running east-west corrugate the land. Gently folded swales divide the
terraces, collecting the meager rainfall and snowmelt that reach this
dry portion of central Colorado. The water moves slowly, pooling in
a cattail marsh, then seeping onward again to join the shallow course
of Fossil Creek. The patch of prairie spreads toward the remaining
horizons, its borders trimmed by rows of houses.

There is just sufficient prairie—1,082 acres—to sense how the
land once looked. Humans set this prairie aside from agriculture and

houses for the benefit of both the life within and the people who live on its borders. Although small, parts of its story reflect that of all the shortgrass prairie once covering the western Great Plains. This story starts at the grassroots; continues through the bustle and brevity of the life of a grasshopper, a prairie dog, and a coyote; and ends on the wings of a hawk riding atmospheric currents that bring the greater world to the prairie. So much happens during the course of a year on this small island of grass that thick chronicles could be written, but this brief narrative provides a glimpse into a year, just as the small prairie island provides a glimpse into the once vast sea of grass.

• • • • • • • • • • • • • • • •

All winter the patch of prairie remains muted, the grasses having died back to straw-colored stubble punctuated only by an occasional yucca or rabbitbrush. Bitterly cold winter winds pit the stubble with hard-driven snow, but the snow seldom lingers. The dry winds sublimate the white crystals or mold them into small drifts in the lee of the bunchgrasses, and within a day or two they are gone. Most creatures are out of sight, but the prairie dogs remain active, their squeaks of alarm sounding when a cruising raptor passes by. Otherwise the landscape waits quietly.

Spring arrives on gusting chinook winds that warm the air, only to be interrupted by arctic winds that can drop the temperature thirty degrees in a few hours. But the warmth gradually wins out as the days grow longer. The entire prairie stirs from its winter of dormancy.

The prairie awakening begins each spring with the greening of the grasses. Everything centers on the grasses. Soil fungi and earthworms live on bits of root and shed plant litter. Caterpillars and grasshoppers eat stem and leaf aboveground. Western meadowlarks and prairie falcons and thirteen-lined ground squirrels pursue the insects, and coyotes and golden eagles swallow rabbits, rodents, and smaller birds with eager appetite.

As the days grow longer during March and April, explosions of green burst across the prairie. Big bluestem surges up from nine-foot-deep roots into gangly seed stalks well over three feet tall. On loose sandy slopes, sand reedgrass sends up coarse stalks to catch the wind with a hiss. Native purple threeawn and invasive prairie threeawn grow slender leaves tapering to a fine point from which narrow, wiry seeds each hold three bristles like long antennae.

The greening grasses survived the lean winter season, when the carbohydrate reserves stored in their roots reach their lowest levels. The plant draws on these reserves throughout the autumn and winter, and if prairie dogs or soil microorganisms eat the portions of the plant that store carbohydrates or if the plant did not store enough sugars and starch in its tissues during the growing season, it will die. Spring regrowth takes a lot of energy, but the payoff comes in new photosynthetic tissue that can replenish the carbohydrate reserves once production exceeds the plant's immediate needs.

The prairie does not green all at once. Patches of new growth appear on the slopes while the lowlands along the small channels remain brown. The early blooms appear. Elegant white clusters of sand lily spring up overnight, and wild parsley blossoms in patches of sunshine yellow. The sepia tones of the winter prairie give way to a broader spectrum of color.

Blue grama is one of the most abundant grass species here. Its slender leaves and seed stalks curl like eyelashes, making the plant

Sand lily in bloom, Fromme Prairie. The white petals grow on short stalks only a couple of inches above the ground.

Seed heads of blue grama grass.

appear tenuous on this prairie of intense sunlight and dessicating winds. Even the species name, *gracilis*, reflects the plant's fragile appearance. But blue grama is a native here, a C_4 plant with metabolic pathways specially adapted to the prairie's warmth, intense sunlight, and periods of water stress. Unlike many plants, it can continue to photosynthesize even when stressed by low moisture levels. The tenacious little blue grama reaches its period of greatest activity in mid- to late summer when air temperatures on the prairie hover between 90° and 100°F at midday.

Some plants avoid dehydration by accumulating water in spongy tissues. Others extend their roots deep into the soil profile until they reach subsurface water. Still others limit water loss from leaves by developing a thick, waxy surface layer or fine hairs that reduce air movement immediately at the leaf surface. Blue grama lacks spongy tissue and a thick leaf surface, and its roots do not extend far downward. Instead, blue grama relies on the ability of its basal stem close to the ground to resist drying. This, along with the roots, forms the vital center of the plant that remains alive during times of stress, and from this vital center new shoots and roots grow when conditions improve. The strength of this vital center increases as the plant ages and is able to store more carbohydrates against lean times.

Grasses appear deceptively simple at the surface—a few green blades, perhaps an inconspicuous flower, or, later, a more readily apparent seed head. This apparent simplicity belies the complex biochemical strategies that allow grasses to survive drought, fire, grazing, limited nutrients, even winter. Unlike animals, which stop growing when they reach maturity, plants continue to grow throughout their entire life span from special tissues in their roots and shoots. In blue grama, this tissue goes dormant during winter and resumes growth in the spring. Most years, some green growth at the leaf tips of blue grama is visible by the first or second week in April. This is the start of the seasonal race. The first leaf or two will mature and die by the end of June. Successive leaves grow longer, and the plant's ability to produce carbohydrates depends on their growth. The longer leaves will reach about a third of their length by the end of May and two-thirds by the end of June. Leaf growth decreases in early July and becomes insignificant by mid-July, hence the race. Blue grama plants have only about three months to grow the photosynthetic surfaces they use to build carbohydrates before the plant above the lower portion of the stem close to the ground dies about mid-September.

Like other grasses, blue grama has two potential ways to reproduce. Asexual reproduction involves no new shuffling of the genetic material of two parent plants. Instead, a single parent sends out genetic copies of itself. Blue grama reproduces asexually by sending out lateral stems just below the ground surface. New shoots grow upward from these lateral stems so that a clump of blue grama grows outward. In a sense, this is a relatively safe way to reproduce because new shoots remain connected to the larger parent plant.

About one in ten of the blue grama shoots that remain dormant through the winter produces flowers for sexual reproduction. Some of these shoots do not flower until their third growing season so that they can store sufficient energy to grow larger and gain a competitive advantage over other shoots. Flowers start to appear at the end of June. Sexual reproduction is riskier because many seeds do not survive germination. Considering in detail the sequence of events needed for successful germination, it seems miraculous that any blue grama survive the first year. The longevity of adult blue grama plants offsets the high mortality of seedlings.

When a grass seed germinates, it first develops a primary root that grows downward from the seed and then additional lateral roots that branch slightly from the primary root below the seed. The primary root of blue grama is seldom longer than four inches. The first critical period for survival of blue grama seedlings occurs immediately, when the soil surface must remain moist for two to four days for seeds to germinate and initiate growth of the primary root. Because the primary root grows less than half an inch each day even under favorable conditions, the soil can dry almost as rapidly as the primary root is growing downward.

The second critical period comes about five to six weeks later, when the primary root begins to deteriorate and progressive downward drying of the soil can get close to the maximum depth of rooting. The plant's ability to absorb water from the soil at this point is limited by the primary root's maximum capacity for water uptake, as well as the soil moisture.

While the primary root grows downward, a seedling grows upward from the seed. The ability of the seed to produce tissues that force a way through the soil is fueled by the production of enzymes that alter the starch and protein stored in the seed into soluble sugars and amino acids the embryo and then the seedling use for growth. All of this is to no avail, however, if the seedling cannot obtain sufficient water.

A third critical period for blue grama seedlings can result from water stress even if the entire primary root is growing in moist soil. The primary root reaches the upper limit of its capacity to absorb water soon after the seedling emerges from the soil, imposing a limit on how much leaf tissue can be kept alive. When seedlings reach these limits, hot, dry winds can cause the seedling to die or reduce the area of green leaves because the rate of water loss from the leaves exceeds the rate of water uptake by the primary root.

The final critical period in the establishment of a blue grama seedling occurs when adventitious roots develop above the seed very close to the ground surface. Because the root system of most mature grass plants consists entirely of adventitious roots, survival of the seedling ultimately depends on its ability to develop those roots. A second moist period of two to four days is required anywhere from two to eight weeks after germination for adventitious roots to initiate growth. Although a blue grama seedling is very resistant to drought and can remain alive for long periods without growing, seedlings that do not develop adventitious roots do not survive the next winter. Yet because the adventitious roots lie less than an inch below the surface, where the soil is dry except during or immediately after a rain or snowmelt, many adventitious roots become dead stubs. Drying of the soil in mid–growing season causes the death of one- to two-thirds of newly formed adventitious roots. Blue grama plants can make up for this with massive root growth during times of moist soil near the end of the growing season.

Blue grama seedlings in effect gamble on the weather. Because temperatures lower than 59°F are inadequate for establishment of adventitious roots, seeds can germinate in early May, when soil temperatures are marginal for root growth but there is a greater chance of two or more consecutive wet days. Or seeds can germinate in midsummer, when soil temperatures are more favorable for seedling emergence and root growth but it becomes less likely that two or more consecutive wet days will occur. Ideal weather conditions for blue grama seed germination and establishment occur infrequently, and this, combined with competition for soil moisture from established adult plants, makes sexual reproduction by blue grama a rare event. This is why croplands that have lain fallow for sixty years at the Central Plains Experimental Range still have no blue grama growing on them.

As with other organisms, neighborhood matters for a blue grama plant struggling to survive its first year. The seedling's immediate environment can determine whether sufficient moisture is available for adventitious roots to grow and survive. Minute variations in the topography of the soil surface, the presence of plant litter, and the presence of neighboring plants all influence the rate at which soil dries. Seedlings do better in the absence of neighboring adult blue grama plants that compete with them for soil moisture. Anything that creates limited gaps in blue grama communities can thus help new seedlings get established.

●　●　●　●　●　●　●　●　●　●　●　●　●　●

As the newly growing asexual shoots of blue grama and the shoots and flowers of other plants begin to appear across the Fromme Prairie in spring, the air takes on new life as well. Wind-ragged flocks of ducks pass overhead, black-headed scaups flashing white wing stripes and redheads showing more subdued gray stripes. The resident Canada geese fly back and forth in tight chevrons. Tiny broad-tailed hummingbirds whir by on their resolute flight to their summer range in the northern mountains. The resident winter raptors—rough-legged hawks, merlins, and bald eagles—catch the migratory urge and turn to the north. Coppery-breasted western bluebirds leave their winter supply of berries and flutter up into the mountains to feed on the insects buzzing in the newfound warmth. The summer residents arrive on the prairie, greeted by the vibrant song of the western meadowlarks that have remained throughout the year. The fluid spring melodies of the meadowlarks promise a richer life, carried on gusts of cold wind while the stirrings of spring are just beginning to drive green rivulets of life into the plants.

The restlessness of the spring air also stirs those who have wintered in the earth. Snakes emerge from their dens hungry for the boreal chorus frogs emerging from the mud of the wetlands. Red foxes and coyotes give birth to young who will eat many a prairie dog and meadow vole and ground squirrel, even as the small rodents give birth to their own young.

The prairie changes swiftly now from week to week. Stalks bearing creamy white flowers rise above the rapidly greening grasses, the beauty of the flowers betrayed by the name "death camas." White flushes of silky locoweed appear. The lengthening hours of sunlight and the spring rains coax the shrubs and sedges and grasses into new sage-green and emerald growth, and the teeming microorganisms of the soil stir themselves into new cycles of activity as the grasses flourish.

Sagebrush, yucca, prickly pear cactus, and rabbitbrush dot the prairie. But the grasses dominate: ricegrass, needlegrass, bluestem, threeawn, grama, saltgrass, wheatgrass, mannagrass, junegrass, muhly, sacaton, dropseed, switchgrass, bluegrass, alkaligrass, indiangrass, cordgrass. More than fifty native species of grass and nearly twenty introduced species bend and twist in the winds that blow nearly constantly across the prairie. Deceptively delicate, the native plants of the short-

Seed heads of buffalo grass.

grass prairie are nonetheless tough survivors that adapt to dry seasons by curling their leaves and closing their stomata. They produce seeds that germinate in dry soil or that remain dormant until a wetter season sets them to sucking up nutrients and growing quickly.

Interspersed among the bunches of blue grama is buffalo grass, another native species adapted to the heat and drought. The tough little grass seldom grows more than half a foot tall, but it sends roots nearly six feet down, hiding its mass from the dessicating air and the grazing animals with which it evolved. Blue grama and buffalo grass are the two characteristic plant species that together define the geographic extent of the shortgrass prairie.

Buffalo grass creates a sod as its lateral stems grow across the ground an inch or two a day until they form a clump more than two feet across. Blue grama appears more contained on the Fromme Prairie, where grazing has not occurred for decades. Each plant forms a bunch separated by other plants or by bare ground. What appear to be separate plants may in fact all be part of one organism that can live at least forty years. A grass plant starts from growth units known as tillers connected to one another at the basal area of the stem. Some tillers produce only leaves; others produce a stem, seed head, roots, and leaves. Differentiation between these two potential pathways depends on environmental conditions. An individual plant can have more than a hundred live tillers. Tillers in the center die as the plant grows broader, until eventually the surface portion of the plant forms discrete clumps. These genetically identical clumps spread slowly, at an inch or less per year, and their apparent isolation from one another led to the name bunchgrasses.

Bunchgrasses form small biological islands in the prairie sea. Like an island that may barely surface above the waves before dropping off into steep slopes that go down fathoms to the ocean bottom, the few inches of blue grama aboveground are only a small portion of the plant. Below the six-inch length of leaves and stems, a dense mat of fibrous roots can tunnel downward to depths of six feet, although the majority of the roots are within half a foot of the soil surface. A plant with a surface area of fifty square inches can have sixteen cubic feet of roots below it. These root masses attract the myriad creatures of the soil, as does the organic litter the plant constantly sheds. Tiny subterranean organisms form the bulk of life on the prairie, making up most of the total mass of living organisms. They are particularly numerous in the first foot of soil, especially the upper few inches. Here the microscopic creatures swarm around plant roots, through the litter of dead plant parts at the surface, and between the clumps of soil below.

The tiniest organisms depend on films of water among the soil particles in order to move and complete their life cycle. A few molecules of water may contain countless bacteria and protozoa, the single-celled animals that eat the bacteria. Also swarming through the water films are the rotifers, wheel animalcules with a circle of minuscule hairs at one end of the body that in motion make the entire organism appear to rotate. In the water films located near plant tissues live the nematodes, tiny roundworms able to consume bacteria or consume up to a quarter of the plant's mass. The nematodes compete with the

Bare soil exposed around bunches of blue grama on the Fromme Prairie.

myccorhizal fungi living in the plant roots. The fungi extract carbon from the roots but also protect them from disease-causing organisms and help the plant take up phosphorus from the soil.

This swarming of minute life serves as the soil chemists and engineers that give soil its fertility by producing organic compounds and tiny rootlets that bind soil particles into clumps. The soil organisms

Bare soil exposed around bunches of blue grama on the Fromme Prairie.

thus form the unacknowledged basis for most life. These creatures, invisible to the human eye, form the critical filter through which most of the plant carbon and soil nutrients must pass.

On one side of this soil filter are the producers, the green plants that capture the energy that fuels the entire complex prairie food web. Chlorophylls in the plants absorb energy from sunlight, combining the energy with water and carbon dioxide to fix carbon into organic compounds such as sugars. Some of these sugars the plants use for their own growth. But as the plants grow, they cast off leaves and twigs and roots, eventually returning almost all of their mass to the soil as dead litter.

On the other side of the soil filter are the consumers. Only a small portion of living plant tissue is consumed aboveground by obvious grazers such as bison and deer. The soil microorganisms consume a much larger portion. As these microorganisms decompose the plant litter, they provide the principal source of nutrients consumed by the plant roots, in effect running a highly efficient recycling system. Microbial activity depends on the temperature and availability of water in the soil and is greater during warm, wet periods when plants are also actively growing. The activity of these tiny grazers in part controls the extent and density of the grassland plants. The microorganisms decomposing the plant litter are in turn consumed by other microbes and larger organisms, which then provide food for higher levels of the food web.

Among the consumers are creatures up to a fraction of an inch long that live within air-filled pore spaces in the soil. These are the insects, nematodes, crustaceans, and mollusks. They are burrowers on a very small scale, enlarging the pores within the soil and recycling organic materials as they move along, eating and excreting.

The smaller burrowers cannot compete with earthworms, though, which are the giants in the earth of this soil kingdom. Some earthworms live in the surface layer of plant litter, steadily shredding the litter in search of the bacteria and fungi that live within it. Other worms go mining down into the deeper, mineral layers of the soil in search of prey, their segmented bodies propelled by wave-like expansions and contractions that push tiny bristles from the worm's skin against the surrounding burrow walls. The industrious worms produce more than half of their body weight in nitrogen-rich urine each day. The fecal pellets they leave behind also provide tiny nuggets of nutrients—concentrated nitrogen, phosphorus, magnesium, potassium, and calcium essential to plant growth. These pellets line the worm burrows, which form pathways through the soil for air and water. Earthworms are the movers and shakers of the soil world, churning, enriching, and aerating the soil.

As an earthworm moves through the subterranean world, it also encounters soil organisms up to a couple of inches long that create their own spaces by burrowing through the soil. These creatures include larger nematodes that eat the smaller ones: beetles, ants, termites, centipedes and millipedes, and other insects. Together these organisms form the upper echelons of the invertebrate food web formed in the biological island around each clump of grass. In these islands a fraction of an ounce of soil may contain more than 1 billion bacteria, 10 to 20 million fungi, up to 3 million algae, 1 million protozoa, fifty nematodes, and perhaps one fat, five-inch-long earthworm.

Live blue grama plants can support more than 100,000 nematodes in a square foot of soil. The nematodes prefer to feed on new roots, but even dead blue grama plants can host more than 18,000 of the little creatures below them. So many mouths eating away belowground poses a challenge for blue grama. Like other plants of the shortgrass prairie, blue grama can adapt to grazing aboveground by storing its nutrients and critical reproductive tissue below the ground surface. These adaptations also enhance the plant's resistance to drought and fire. Consumption of plant tissue by ruminant animals such as cattle and bison and by insects living above the ground takes about a third of the plant's production in moderately grazed areas. Consumption of plant tissue belowground can be more serious because it interferes with the plant's ability to maintain adequate water supplies during periods when water is limited, as well as interfering with storage of nutrients and plant reproduction.

Fortunately for blue grama, consumption of plant tissue by nematodes and other soil dwellers is just over 10 percent of the plant's production most of the time. This percentage can rise, however, during population booms of soil organisms. Root-feeding white grubs, the larvae of a May beetle, experience an outbreak every ten years or so, during which the grubs can reduce the plant's production of roots and shoots by as much as 60 percent. The contest is not all one-sided, however; changes in the roots can also reduce nematode density, although it remains unclear whether the nematodes die or enter a quiescent state. Nematodes can survive periods of low soil moisture by entering a state with little or no metabolic activity and then become active again when conditions become favorable. They may wait out reductions in their food supply of roots in a similar manner.

Populations of bacteria feeding on blue grama roots also fluctuate with time. Bacteria can be particularly abundant among the dying roots of drought-stressed plants and in springtime when new root growth provides a source of carbon for the bacteria. Populations of microbivores, which feed on bacteria, rise and fall with the bacteria, as do seasonal trends in predatory nematodes that feed on the microbivores. Everything centers on the grasses.

• • • • • • • • • • • • • • • •

This stable, self-sustaining soil ecosystem so vital with minute organisms is a self-renewing treasure trove giving forth all that we delight in, from morning light on a newly opened wild violet to the warble of a meadowlark fed on insects. The ability of this treasure to renew itself ultimately rests on the exchanges of carbon.

Carbon is one of the elements fundamental to living organisms. Along with five other elements, carbon makes up 99 percent of all living tissue. The photosynthesizers fix carbon in a form usable by other organisms. All the other creatures then trade the carbon, each briefly storing the carbon in its own tissues and assembling it with associated nutrients to build the carbohydrates, lipids, and proteins that reassemble to create the tissue of a fungus, a springtail, or an earthworm.

Carbon uptake varies with the species of plant and the specific local conditions. Blue grama can absorb up to one hundredth (0.01) of an ounce of carbon dioxide per square foot of leaf area each hour in the middle of June following a good rain. Uptake rates decrease as the soil dries out, reaching a low of one thousandth (0.001) of an ounce of carbon dioxide per square foot in mid-July. Photosynthesis by blue grama tends to be most efficient at temperatures of 93–97°F when not severely limited by available water. The optimum temperature for photosynthesis increases by 3–7°F when the plant is water-stressed, meaning blue grama becomes more efficient at the higher temperatures likely to be present during dry times. This is another indication of blue grama's adaptation to the heat and dryness of the western plains.

Blue grama shifts carbon within its tissues as the plant's needs change. One pool of carbon is located in the aboveground portions of the plant, typically the leaves. Another pool of carbon is temporarily stored in the base of stems and the upper roots. This pool is typically used by the plant at the beginning of the growing season and is later replenished by transfer of carbon from the photosynthesizing leaves. As might be expected, carbohydrate concentrations in the tissues of blue grama are lowest early in the spring and highest late in the growing season. The plant can also shift some of its carbon storage between leaves and roots in response to grazing aboveground or belowground.

At any given time, living organisms contain only a small fraction of the total carbon stored in soil. Recently dead or decomposing plants and animals form about half of the soil carbon. The remainder is the soil humus, the organic compounds too chemically complex to be used by most organisms or hidden away in tight clumps of soil particles. The different components of humus may reside in the soil for tens to hundreds of years before being released from the soil or taken up by living organisms.

The carbon exchanges carried out among the soil plants and animals form one component of a broader carbon cycle that extends up into the atmosphere. This greater carbon cycle is highly influenced by the fact that the soil carbon cycle leaks. When soil animals shred plant litter into smaller sizes, microorganisms consume portions of the shredded tissue. During this microorganismal feast, carbon is lost from the soil as carbon dioxide diffusing back into the atmosphere. Progressively more carbon is lost in the form of carbon dioxide as the remaining carbon is cycled among the different soil organisms. Much of the carbon, however, is assimilated into microbial tissue or converted into stable humus. Because of these storage mechanisms, soil contains the greatest surface reservoir of carbon on the planet, exceeding the carbon held in other living organisms by six to ten times.

Humans are rightly concerned about increases in atmospheric greenhouse gases resulting from our fossil fuel consumption. But the devil is in the seemingly unconnected details. Clearing the shortgrass prairie for cropland or houses—such as on the edges of the Fromme Prairie—may increase greenhouse gases if the change in plant species and soil dynamics results in more carbon dioxide being lost from the carbon reservoir formed by grassland soils than can be taken out of the air by the plants.

Grassland soils also store nitrogen, another component of greenhouse gases. As with carbon, the soil reservoir can leak nitrogen to the atmosphere through surface runoff or erosion, chemical reactions in the soil, or, most important, the actions of microbes. The fixation or removal of nitrogen by microbes is the primary control over the emission of nitric and nitrous oxide gases to the atmosphere. Although emissions of these gases are a small fraction of the total nitrogen cycle, they play a major role in atmospheric chemistry. Nitrous oxide has a long residence time in the atmosphere, persisting on average for more than 100 years. On a per molecule basis, nitrous oxide is 200 times as effective at trapping heat as carbon dioxide; a little nitrous oxide goes a long way toward contributing to greenhouse warming. Further nitrogen may be released once the climate warms because emissions of nitrous oxide from soil increase with temperature. Soil ecology of grasslands thus becomes of fundamental importance not only for the grassland communities but also for the global community.

The entire basis for the amount of leakage from the soil reservoir—the organic content of the soil and its carbon and nitrogen storage—is controlled by many factors that differ across a patch of landscape as small as the Fromme Prairie. The input from plant litter and animal dung is critical, as are the pathways by which this material is cycled through the soil food web. If plant litter has much more carbon than nitrogen, the community of decomposers will deplete levels of nitrogen in the soil in the course of processing the litter. Dung from grazing animals, on the other hand, has carbon and nitrogen proportions more favorable for the fixation of nitrogen. The moist dung is rich habitat for decomposers, and microorganisms from the animals' digestive systems continue to be active in the dung. Dung thus contributes nitrogen to the soil nitrogen reservoir.

Dung also influences how individual plants succeed one another through time. Plants die because they stored too few carbohydrate reserves to live off during periods of stress such as drought or winter. Ants kill plants by removing growth tissue below the soil surface on and around the ant nest. Burrowing animals kill plants by mounding soil over them or removing the plants while digging. Small plants such as blue grama also die when cow dung completely covers the plant and prevents photosynthesis. Cow dung can cover a space nearly ten inches across, about the same size as a blue grama plant, and can take more than six years to decay in this dry environment. What a way to go. Yet the gap formed by the death of one plant provides a germination site for another plant, maintaining a dynamic community in which patches of individual plants change across space and time.

Water and soil texture also play a vital role in controlling soil processes. Although average air temperature and precipitation are consistent across the Fromme Prairie, south-facing surfaces hold the warmth of the winter sunlight longer than surfaces facing other directions. Rainfall and snowmelt do not drain as swiftly from swales or flats. The drier the site, the sparser the plant cover and the lower the biomass of soil invertebrates. Wet soils in cattail marshes have a

Dried cow dung amid blue grama plants, Pawnee National Grassland. Bunch of keys at left on cow dung for scale.

different community of microorganisms that produce different metabolic products and a slower rate of organic matter decomposition than the dry, sandy soils on ridgetops. Soils on the crest of hillslopes tend to lose mass to erosion. The toe of a slope captures this eroding mass and develops thick, rich accumulations of soil. Carbon, nitrogen, and phosphorus content of the soil all increase downslope from a ridge crest to a swale as soil clay content and moisture increase.

The time over which a portion of ground has been stable and a soil has been forming also plays a role in soil organic content. A surface recently exposed after a sand dune moved across it, or newly created by a fresh load of river silt and sand, will have relatively low organic content.

Finally, the bedrock weathering into unconsolidated particles that form the soil foundation partially controls the organic content. The smaller denizens of the soil choose their homes in part based on the underlying rock type. Side by side in the dry climate of the Fromme Prairie, a shale weathers more rapidly than a sandstone, producing more silt and clay-sized particles than the sandy soils weathered from the sandstone. Sand, silt, and clay have different abilities to hold and transmit soil water, which in turn create different surface plant and soil microorganism communities. What appears as a uniform landscape at the broadest focus on closer examination resolves into a mosaic of local differences in soil carbon cycling and storage reflected in different soil microorganisms and plant associations.

* * * * * * * * * * * * * * * *

The soils on the Fromme Prairie are mostly underlain by shale, an impermeable but brittle rock formed from hardened clays. Sixty-five million years ago this region was the edge of a shallow sea forming part of the Cretaceous Interior Seaway. Deltas and estuaries formed along the coast, and mud carried downstream from the western mountains to the sea was gradually buried by more and more sediment. The pressure and heat of deep burial eventually hardened the mud into shale, which was then carried upward when a later period of mountain building to the west lifted the prairie region a mile above sea level. Now the shale gradually weathers once more into sediment in the inexorable turns of the rock cycle, and the presence of this fine-grained rock is the starting point for all of the soil characteristics that control the presence of plants and animals.

Shale returns to silt and clay as it weathers. Mixed with the silt, clay, and sand that the wind blows in and the sediments brought down by the rivers, the weathered shale forms loamy soils. Well-drained soils form on the uplands, and deep, poorly drained clay soils form in the valley bottoms. A blue grama seed recognizes these differences, as does a grasshopper laying eggs in the soil and a prairie dog digging a burrow.

Differences in water availability and soil texture produce a high diversity of plant species. It is hard to perceive from a rapid screening of the apparently consistent vegetation on the Fromme Prairie, but on this 1,082-acre fragment grow 28 native species of trees and shrubs, 141 native wildflowers and other broadleaf herbs, and 54 native grasses. The distribution of these plants across the prairie's uplands and valleys reflects not only the soils and microclimates but also the competition between different plant and animal species. By their location and type, plants record the history of this landscape.

Changes large and small mark the history of the prairie. Drought-adapted plants have waxed and waned on the grasslands over tens of thousands of years as the climate warmed and cooled. During the past 10,000 years, the regional climate occasionally became sufficiently hot and dry to allow sand dunes to form in parts of eastern Colorado. Most recently, the drought of the 1930s Dust Bowl killed off all but the most drought-tolerant species of the shortgrass plant communities.

Superimposed on the drought cycles are periodic scorchings by fire. Fire consumes the surface plant litter, releasing the nutrients stored within. The newly exposed soil warms earlier in the spring, and sites are opened for new plant growth. Prairie dogs come to the recently burned sites in search of preferred plants, and their grazing and burrowing further alter the soil and the plant communities.

Human uses of the land also alter the plant communities. The Fromme Prairie was lightly grazed by cattle and horses over the past 100 years. Remnants of the foundation of an old brick factory, a few utility poles, and groundwater testing wells are present. In places the landscape has been contoured for stock ponds and irrigation ditches. A heavily used concrete path meanders east-west across the prairie near Fossil Creek, and installation of utility pipes for new housing developments along the prairie's northern boundary ripped a broad swath north-south across its center. In each of these places where the native plants were disrupted by human activities, invasive plant species can gain a roothold.

Invasive plants are those introduced to an environment in which they did not evolve. These plants have fewer natural enemies to limit their reproduction and spread compared with native species. The successful invaders also have strategies that allow them to out-compete other plants. They mature early and reproduce profusely. They produce biological toxins that suppress the growth of other plants. Spines that repel grazing animals cover them. They photosynthesize at high rates or parasitize other plants. They spread quickly by way of runners or through seeds that stick to animals or drift far on the winds. Their seeds can endure long periods of dormancy in the soil until conditions are right for germination. They are vegetable prodigies.

The introduced invaders have displaced approximately 10 percent of Colorado's 1,500 species of native plants. On the Fromme Prairie, Russian olive and Siberian elm threaten the native cottonwood and willow species in the wetlands. Bromes and fescues from Asia and Europe compete with the native buffalo grass, blue grama, little bluestem, and needle-and-thread grass. The problem with the invasives is that a change in plant species composition ripples through the entire grassland ecosystem, lowering its ability to support diverse and abundant life.

The islands of blue grama and associated native species attract soil organisms because of the organic litter the plants produce. The aboveground portions of the grass make the ground surface rougher, slowing the flow of wind and rainwater runoff and collecting some of the sediments these currents transport. When the plant dies, it creates a flush of organic matter and nutrients that lasts for several months or even years.

The invasive species, by contrast, contribute less organic matter near the soil surface. Their thick taproots decompose more slowly than the fine grass roots. Because they take up soil nutrients rapidly or tolerate low levels of nutrients, they deplete the soil's reserves of nitrogen, potassium, and phosphorus. Their deeper roots exploit the entire depth of soil for water and nutrients, but these materials

Needle-and-thread grass, Fromme Prairie.

are not cycled through the soil food web because invasive forbs and shrubs produce chemicals that hinder soil microorganisms from feeding on their living roots and slow the decomposition of their dead roots. Where invasive shrubs replace grasses, the shrubs are less effective at protecting the soil from raindrop erosion or creating surface roughness that traps snowflakes and allows meltwater to soak into the ground. Consequently, the exposed soil becomes crusted, and water runs downslope at the surface rather than soaking in. Shallow-rooted seedlings have a harder time becoming established as the soil dries. The dry soil exposed to the air has larger fluctuations in temperature. The soil particles clump together less well. The end result is decreases in community productivity and in the number of species and the abundance of each species.

Nobody loves a weed, but it is difficult not to admire the ingenuity and tenacity of these invasive plants. Dalmatian toadflax, leafy spurge, and cheat grass are among the plants that have invaded the

Fromme Prairie. Introduced to the West Coast of North America from the Mediterranean in 1874 as an ornamental plant and a source of fabric dye and folk remedies, Dalmatian toadflax is not vulnerable to the competition and soil moisture that limit most plants. A single toadflax can produce up to 500,000 seeds a year that the wind effectively disperses. The toadflax is the "early bird," regenerating from vegetative buds on its root stock early each spring before the other plants get going.

Leafy spurge was brought to northeastern North America from Eurasia as an ornamental in 1829. It now infests close to 3 million acres in twenty-nine states. This long-lived perennial has such high genetic variability that it easily adapts to local growing conditions. Each flowering stem produces more than 100 seeds, and exploding seed capsules project these seeds up to fifteen feet from the parent plant. These are superseeds. They can float on water, survive animal digestive tracts, and remain viable for eight years or more. If the seeds are not enough, rootbuds up to ten feet belowground can each produce a new plant. Once a seedling gets started it can outstrip competitors, sending roots three feet down and nearly two feet to each side in four months. A mature plant has roots to depths of twenty-six feet spreading fifteen feet laterally.

Cheat grass seems to line every road and pathway in the dry grasslands of the western United States. It now occupies about 100 million acres, approximately 20 percent of the sagebrush and grasslands in the region. A cool season annual grass introduced from Eurasia, cheat grass grows during the fall and early spring, gaining a competitive advantage over the slower-growing, native perennial plants. Cheat grass seeds can remain viable for as long as five years, and some of the estimated $2 billion in economic losses associated with cheat grass each year comes from contamination of winter wheat dryland seedbanks with cheat grass seeds. Cheat grass can out-compete native species in disturbed environments, and it thrives on fire. The fine stalks and seeds dry out earlier during the growing season than do native plants, which contributes to increased fire frequency and intensity that kill off native species without limiting the cheat grass.

An undisturbed native prairie can resist many invasive species despite their competitive advantages. But any disturbance provides a potential roothold for the weeds. Because of its limited ability to

Leafy spurge growing along a trail, Fromme Prairie.

reproduce sexually, blue grama is very slow to recolonize disturbed sites; further, established blue grama has a limited ability to exploit resources more than a few inches beyond its canopy. The great majority of its roots lie beneath the plant, although some extend more than a foot away. Blue grama has not managed to reestablish across about 5 million acres of abandoned cropland during the forty to fifty years since cultivation ceased. Weeds have taken over many of these acres.

Cheat grass growing beside a concrete path, Fromme Prairie.

Both native animals and cattle decline to eat many of the invasive exotic plants, but other methods of controlling invasives are available. Biological weed management can be used, with insects, pathogens, or nematodes to target individual species, but care must be taken that the biological agent will attack only the weeds and not other plants. Selective herbicides can preferentially destroy the weeds, but it is becoming increasingly clear that any chemical harmful to one living organism is also likely to harm other organisms. Pulling, burning, mowing, or hoeing the weeds; mulching the ground to smother them; fertilizing to help native plants become established on disturbed ground; and replanting with desirable species are all possible means of control. At present, managers of natural areas practice limited weed control on the Fromme Prairie.

As the weeds spread, they deplete the prairie's reservoir of soil wealth by rapidly using nutrients without returning much plant litter to the soil. In this respect, the weeds create an effect similar to heavy grazing or cropping. These disturbances reduce the uptake of carbon and increase the emission of nitrous oxide, contributing to greenhouse warming. The grassland ecosystem's long-stored and carefully recycled pool of carbon, nitrogen, and other nutrients takes several decades to reaccumulate once a disturbance such as farming ceases. Farming or overgrazing the shortgrass prairie is thus a form of mining because it depletes the soil nutrients at a much greater rate than they can be naturally replenished.

For a human walking across the prairie, the landscape may appear lifeless except for plants and the larger creatures such as birds that eat worms. A handful of the powdery dry, pale-colored soil may also appear lifeless except for the occasional worm. Because of our inability to see most of the soil's inhabitants, we miss the real activity and accept soil fertility as some kind of benevolent magic unconnected to our activities. But we can alter the complex exchange of nutrients among the interconnected components of the soil food web by changing the species of plants and animals present on the prairie or by adding poisons that kill some of the soil organisms. Expecting soil fertility to persist in the wake of such alterations is like expecting a few surviving humans to fully reconstruct a complex urban civilization in the wake of a catastrophe.

* * * * * * * * * * * * * * * *

The entire complex world through which small rotifers and earthworms move is the thinnest of skins. Most of the soil microorganisms live within a foot of the surface. The plant roots punch down through this organic-rich layer into the mineral soil or the fractured bedrock below, but even the roots seldom extend more than ten feet below the surface. The burrows of prairie dogs may go down another few feet, but on the Fromme Prairie prairie dogs likely hit the bedrock of the Pierre Shale formation at depths of ten or twenty feet. In places the bedrock may lie more deeply buried beneath sands and gravels carried down by rivers draining the mountains to the west, but seldom is the rock surface more than twenty feet down.

Rocks record history, but they sometimes leave mysterious gaps. Although the younger sedimentary rocks produced by erosion and deposition from the third generation of ancestral mountains are present on the plains of eastern Colorado, they are missing on the flanks of the mountains along the Fromme Prairie. Between 20 and 5 million years ago, the latest episode of mountain uplift so energized the streams draining east from the Rockies that they eroded these sedimentary rocks. This erosion left a 63-million-year gap in the geological record between the Pierre Shale and the overlying sediments deposited within the last 2 million years.

Below the Pierre Shale lies a sequence of layered sedimentary rocks 8,000 feet thick. These are the deposits of ancient shallow seas, deltas, and alluvial fans that preceded today's rolling prairie lands. Beneath the sedimentary rocks lie the ancient crystalline rocks of the basement. But even this 30-mile-thick crust is only the skin above unimaginably thick molten layers below. Underneath the crust, currents slowly convect through the mantle, a partially molten layer 1,740 miles thick. The mantle is the source for the plumes of liquefied rock surging up through the surface as volcanic eruptions or cooling more slowly in a subterranean bulge that, through the processes of mountain building and erosion, is eventually exposed as the granitic mass of mountains such as the Colorado Rockies. Below the mantle lie another 2,080 miles of the Earth's dense core. The decay of radioactive elements in this core provides the heat that slowly churns upward through the mantle, cracking the brittle layer of the planet's crust into plates that move about through time.

•   •   •   •   •   •   •   •   •   •   •   •   •   •   •

All of the processes of erosion and deposition, so vital to the viability of plants and animals, occupy much less than 1 percent of the planet's

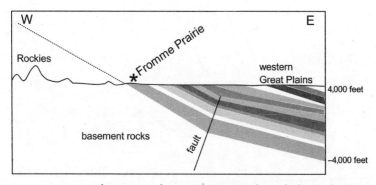

Schematic geologic cross-section through the Rocky Mountains and western Great Plains. Individual rock units, here shown as different shades of gray, dip toward the east and, if projected upward to the west (dotted line), indicate the former elevation of the mountains. Elevations above sea level shown at right; the vertical scale is greatly exaggerated in this view.

depth. The nematodes and blue grama and coyotes live on much less than 1 percent of *that* 1 percent on the Fromme Prairie.

The prairie holds an almost inconceivably thin skin of life over unimaginably immense depths of dark, lifeless rock. Perhaps it is good that most creatures focus on the immediacy of life. A butterfly and a funnel-web weaver spider each lives only one season. A red-tailed hawk may live eighteen years. Both a short-horned lizard and a prairie dog may live five years. The life of a rabbit, a vole, or a darkling beetle is over within two years; a pronghorn antelope may persist for a decade. Even the longest-lived individual occupies but a fleeting moment of the deep geological time through which the landscape evolves.

Likewise, for each individual, space does not scale with time. The boreal chorus frog will likely live its five years within one acre at a pond. The five years of the red fox will be spread across a sixty-five-acre home range. Further, the features on which an organism is focused do not scale with the perceptions of other living creatures who share the same relative space and time. Subtle differences in soil moisture that guide an earthworm during its ten years of slow, churning progress pass largely unnoticed by a coyote loping across its twenty-five-mile range during those same ten years. Even the seventy

View west across the Fromme Prairie from the top of a stream terrace. The house at right is built atop another terrace above the creek at the rear-center of the view.

years of a human life can be insufficient to reveal the complex lives and biochemical cycles constantly churning in the prairie soil. To a human bicycling or jogging across the prairie, perhaps wearing headphones, the prairie appears bland and simple. The views are long, intruded only at the edges where housing divisions hem in the prairie.

Beneath the feet of oblivious humans, the blue grama and buffalo grass green, set seed, and die back to their roots during the winter. As the prairie greens with spring, some of the plant carbon is consumed by earthworms and carried deep into the soil. Some is eaten by prairie dogs and cottontail rabbits and dispersed by the highly mobile animals. Some forms a meal for a brownspotted grasshopper, and the carbon atoms from the rooted grass move into a different portion of the prairie's food web.

LIFE AMONG THE LEAVES OF GRASS

*I would be converted to a religion of grass. Sleep the
winter away and rise headlong with each spring. Sink
deep roots. Conserve water. Respect and nourish your
neighbors.*

—**LOUISE ERDRICH***

The brownspotted grasshopper, *Psoloessa delicatula*, is just starting its second summer of life on the Fromme Prairie. Adult female
brownspotted grasshoppers laid their eggs the preceding summer in
patches of bare ground. Drilling inch-deep holes into the soil with
their abdomens, they deposited eggs that began to hatch in early July.
Meanwhile, it is open season on the eggs. Tiny red mites feed on
them. Nematodes, flies, and beetles find them tasty. Snakes, shrews,

---

* Louise Erdrich, "Big Grass (Northern Tallgrass Prairie, North Dakota),"
  in J. Barbato and L. Weinerman, eds., *Heart of the Land: Essays on Last Great
  Places* (New York: Pantheon Books, 1994), 149.

mice, and moles might devour an entire egg mass if they come across it in their burrowing. Any eggs that survive this predation produce nymphs that resemble miniature adults without wings. The newly hatched nymphs have about four months aboveground during their first season. During this period they repeatedly shed their exoskeleton and grow from two-tenths of an inch to nearly half an inch in body length.

As with the time of developing as eggs in the soil, the nymphal period is a dangerous one. The nymphs are sensitive to the changeable summer weather, and a heavy rain can kill many of them. The tiny, flightless insects emerge into a complex microlandscape of grasses and shrubs. Mostly, the nymphs find a nourishing bunch of blue grama or buffalo grass and stay put. Eating and avoiding those who would eat them occupy the nymphs full-time. Leaping from grass blade to grass blade, the nymphs might move less than 300 feet over a six-week period. This is a reasonable strategy to avoid predators such as the big black tiger beetles, which prey on other insects or scavenge their dead bodies. This beetle assumes its role early in life, its larvae snatching small insects that wander by its underground burrow.

Cold weather in November sends the grasshopper nymphs into shelter under leaf litter or at shallow depths in the soil for a winter of dormancy. Spells of unseasonably warm weather during the winter coax a few individuals into renewed activity for brief periods, but mostly the nymphs wait. Psoloessa and the other species of grasshopper eggs and nymphs resume development with the warmth of spring and emerge to eat the newly sprouting blue grama and other grasses.

A grasshopper's view among native bunchgrasses, Fromme Prairie.

Imagine a world filled with food towering overhead that is longer than you are when cut down. The little Psoloessa has two means of attacking the problem. She can climb a short distance up the leaf, cut the leaf by eating through it, and then, while clinging to the base of the leaf with her mid- and hind legs, hold onto the cut portion with her front legs and feed on the entire leaf to the tip. This would be almost like a human eating an enormous ear of corn while clinging to a telephone pole. Or she can remain on the ground, raise her head and cut through the leaf—felling it like a lumberjack—pick up the fallen leaf, then feed on it from the cut end to the tip. She can also take the seemingly easier way out, by feeding on ground litter and on attached leaves of grass that are recumbent rather than upright.

Spring's unsettled weather keeps Psoloessa's daily activity sporadic for the first week or two after she emerges. Bright days when the temperature climbs above 80°F foreshadow the coming summer. Then a front moves down from the Arctic, and two inches of wet, heavy snow temporarily shut down all the newly resuming growth on the prairie. Only the wind is constant. Cold blasts from the northwest that seem about to sweep the prairie down to barren sand dunes can suddenly still overnight and be replaced by equally forceful gusts that seem gentler because they carry warmth from the south. The great masses of air redistributing energy as the planet tilts about its axis come to the prairie as winds that mirror the exuberance of life in spring.

Above the grassy terrain occupied by Psoloessa, the returning warmth and growing plants also coax the insects of the air to renewed activity. Like Psoloessa, some of them wait out the season of cold and darkness in a state of suspended animation, dormant in the soil or under plant litter. This strategy conserves energy but leaves the organism vulnerable to a period of intense cold or foraging by an animal that remains active during winter. Other species migrate to the bounty of warmer climates, risking a variety of hazards en route and using tremendous energy reserves for the journey. Either strategy has drawbacks, yet plenty of individuals survive to repopulate the prairie each spring.

Wonderful magic: insects and birds appearing singly and in small groups from lands far distant or emerging from hidden refuges within this exposed environment where diminutive bunches of grass seem to offer no real shelter from the continual wind and intense sunlight. Yet here they are once more, their successive appearances recording the progression of time as reliably as dates ticked off a calendar.

Perhaps the most amazing are the butterflies, the epitome of fragile beauty with their rainbow-hued wings thin as tissue paper yet able to migrate thousands of miles each year. During the course of the summer, sixty species of butterflies live out their brief lives on the prairie. The life of a butterfly is as evanescent as the morning dew. As with many insects, the adult stage most visible to humans forms only the briefest portion of the animal's life cycle. Once the female glues her masses of eggs to the underside of a leaf or stem, she dies. Choice of a host plant is not random. Spring whites prefer to breed on introduced alyssum or native hairy rockcress or Carolina draba, whereas the pallid tiger swallowtails seek out Arkansas or woods roses or the American plum. By choosing the right plants on which to lay their eggs, the butterflies ensure that their hungry caterpillars feed well at the expense of the host plant. The eggs hatch into caterpillars that eat voraciously, repeatedly molting over a period of three to six weeks until each remaining caterpillar finds a sheltered site in the grass or plant litter and spins a silk cocoon. Within about ten days, or in some species after the passage of one winter, the adult emerges, to live for less than a month. By comparison, Psoloessa might enjoy a long life.

The dry air of the prairie cools rapidly once the sun sets each day. Psoloessa spends each chilly night sheltering under grass litter, not emerging until three hours after sunrise. She needs another three hours of warming in the sun to raise her body temperature sufficiently for activity. Orienting her long, narrow body so her side faces the sun, Psoloessa basks and feeds a little on ground litter. Meanwhile the soil temperature climbs above 70°F, even though the air temperature an inch above the ground remains just over 50°F. Psoloessa finally gets down to the job of felling giant grass blades late in the morning. She eats steadily until midafternoon, when cooling temperatures again send her into basking mode until she takes cover for the evening a couple of hours later.

Even this truncated daily activity is sufficient to bring Psoloessa to adulthood by May. Well camouflaged in shades of brown, cream, and tan, her body is now six-tenths of an inch long and includes wings that extend beyond the end of her abdomen. Although she continues to spend much of her time on the ground and has to bask for three to four hours after sunrise before she can fly, the wings prove highly useful for evading predators.

Psoloessa's mother had laid her eggs in the bare ground within a colony of black-tailed prairie dogs. As Psoloessa and her siblings grow larger, the grasshoppers find the prairie dog colony a less congenial home. The bare ground that had been an advantage for laying eggs later makes the grasshoppers more visible, and plenty of guests invite themselves to the grasshopper feast. There is danger from the air—kestrels and merlins, screech and barn owls, Swainson's hawks, plovers, meadowlarks, and grasshopper sparrows. Danger lurks on the ground in the form of burrowing owls, coyotes, skunks, toads, prairie dogs, and ground squirrels. Barely visible danger comes from parasitic robber flies, the same tiny red mites that eat the grasshopper eggs, and wasps that sting the grasshoppers—storing the paralyzed prey in their nests as food for young wasps. Although the prairie dog town had significantly higher densities of grasshoppers than the surrounding land during the spring, the situation is reversed by late summer.

To these threats Psoloessa responds with camouflage, minimal movement during much of the day, and flight. When fleeing danger, Psoloessa's wings do not make the clicking sound so often heard during grasshopper flight, and her path can be fairly erratic, covering five to nine feet at heights of four to six inches above the ground. At the end of each flight a quick turn in direction and a sudden drop to the ground can confuse the pursuing hunter. Although Psoloessa does not migrate like some other species of grasshopper, her wings can also help her disperse to better habitat if necessary; brownspotted grasshoppers have been found up to a mile away from suitable habitat.

Psoloessa shares the Fromme Prairie with many other types of grasshoppers. Although grasshopper species have not been inventoried at the prairie, the Central Plains Experimental Range (CPER) includes at least fifty-nine species of orthopterans—grasshoppers, crickets, and locusts. Like Psoloessa, some species are relatively sedentary. Others, like the well-named migratory grasshopper, have a wider range. Some emerge as nymphs early in the growing season, others emerge later, but they all emerge ready to consume plants to fuel their own growth. The relationship among these insects and the prairie plants is more complicated, however, than a simple, one-way plant-to-insect flow of materials and energy.

Because grasshoppers are one of the dominant insect groups in grasslands in terms of numbers of both species and individuals, they have the potential to substantially affect grassland plant communities by eating a lot of plant tissues. As might be expected, at least some plants have evolved deterrents to grasshopper grazing in the form of alkaloids in the flowers and foliage. Common forbs such as prairie coneflower, Colorado locoweed, scarlet globemallow, and plains larkspur can deter grasshopper grazing with these compounds, even though cattle happily consume many of these plants.

The saliva of some insects, however, actually stimulates plant growth. Diligent ecologists have found that some plants regrow more quickly after being grazed by insects than after being mechanically clipped, although this is not always the case. Blue grama grows more slowly after being grazed by lubber grasshoppers, for example. The different responses may reflect different movement patterns by grazers. If the grazers move on after eating a plant, then it makes evolutionary sense for the plant to regrow quickly so it can go on producing sugars to store for its own use during winter. But if the grazers remain nearby, the plant does better not to regrow too quickly.

Even if the grazing grasshopper's saliva exerts no chemical influence on plant growth, the process of removing plant tissue causes a series of complex responses within the plant. After grazing, blue grama puts out a greater proportion of shoots than roots. Blue grama and other plants continually shift carbon and nitrogen among their different tissues. Normally, about 80 percent of the nitrogen taken up by the roots is sent to the shoots, even as carbon taken up by the leaves during photosynthesis is being transferred to the roots. When something eats the plant roots or shoots, these processes are affected. Belowground grazing by nematodes, for example, cuts in half the amount of nitrogen going up to the shoots, so shoot growth also declines. Grasshoppers obviously have a different effect if their grazing causes the shoots to grow more. Two changes seem to explain this. First, grasshoppers, like other eaters, are not completely efficient. They use some of the energy stored in plant tissue for their own growth, but they also excrete some in their feces, which soil microorganisms promptly recycle. Grasshoppers also drop some of the plants they clip, increasing leaf litter. Both of these processes can increase the availability of nitrogen in the soil. Second, removal of shoots decreases the supply of carbon to the plant and thus to the roots. In response, the blue grama mobilizes material from its internal structures into a pool on which it can draw for metabolism and increase its photosynthesis and uptake of carbon. The plant's ability to respond to grazing depends in part on other conditions; for example, blue grama suffers more from intense grazing in dry years than in wetter years.

As the intensity of aboveground grazing by either grasshoppers or larger herbivores such as cattle increases, some optimum is reached beyond which the blue grama cannot keep pace. Consumption by grasshoppers is generally on the order of 10 percent of the production by plants, but it can vary widely. Individual grasshoppers eat more at warmer temperatures and preferentially eat younger plants.

Dusky grasshopper on the concrete path across
the Fromme Prairie in early autumn.

Most grasshoppers reach their greatest density at a site immediately
after eggs hatch, but maximum grazing intensity occurs later, when
they become adults. The amount grasshoppers eat also depends on
the body size of each species; grasshopper species with medium to
large bodies consume up to four times as much as small-bodied grasshoppers. Some grasshopper species experience periodic population
explosions during which the insects can chew off so much vegetation
that is not actually eaten that litter production equals a third of the
total standing vegetation. When blue grama production can no longer keep pace with grasshopper consumption, the insects must move
on; this is one reason migration evolved on the shortgrass prairie.

. . . .

Not all animal inhabitants of the prairie find it necessary to migrate,
of course; some manipulate the environment around them to create
optimal conditions. Among the more effective manipulators are the
western harvester ants. From the place where Psoloessa emerged as
a nymph, a smooth slope angles gently south toward a small creek.

Here and there the low, broad mound of a prairie dog burrow or the sharper, narrower cone of an ant mound pocks the slope. At about a foot high and two feet wide, the ant mounds easily blend into the vegetation from a distance despite being surrounded by a ring of bare ground. Each mound lacks an obvious hole or central opening, but at least a few ants crawl about over the mound and in the vicinity during daylight hours from spring through autumn. A layer of tiny, carefully sorted pebbles that help keep the finer soil of the interior moist covers each mound. Beneath these pebbles the intricately layered galleries of the ant colony twine down into the soil.

These galleries reflect feats of engineering as impressive as human constructions. A colony of harvester ants can occupy a nest for six decades, and during this time the ants modify the soil characteristics so effectively that soils in the nest are less dense, more able to absorb rainfall and melting snow, and richer in organic matter than the surrounding soils.

Each ant colony is founded by a queen, a fertile female who continues to lay eggs for many years after her single mating. These eggs grow into larvae, cocooned pupae, and finally new queens; into infertile female workers and soldiers; or into short-lived males that die after their annual mating flight. Each colony contains from a few dozen to more than half a million ants, all the product of one mother. The ants' primary jobs are to collect and store the seeds they eat during the winter and to tend the prodigious output of their common mother until the young ones can join the ranks of workers. From their base of operations, the ants create and maintain trails that radiate out toward the plants that supply them with seed to eat. Hungry harvester ants remove all the seeds from preferred plant species. One scientist recorded foragers from a single harvester ant nest removing up to 1,600 seeds in a day.

Members of the ant colony inhibit plant growth on the mound by clipping vegetation at the soil surface, and if something causes the nest to become shaded the ants will relocate. The ants also remove the vegetation in a circle around the mound, although it is not clear whether they do this to regulate the mound's temperature or to make it easier for ants outside the nest to avoid predators or to move about. Whatever the cause, the effect is attractive to many other plants and animals. Blue grama, for example, grows more densely around ant mounds than in adjacent areas. Once the ant colony abandons a site, however, forbs, succulents, and shrubs revegetate the mound first. Scientists estimate that 140 years must pass before blue grama becomes the dominant plant on the abandoned mound.

One of the sources of mortality for blue grama is new ant colonies. Each queen of a mature colony produces as many as 300 new queens every year. Each of these new queens is capable of starting a new colony, although few actually succeed in establishing a full-sized nest with a stable population. Although ants from each nest denude only a tiny fraction of the surroundings, disturbed soil attracts ant queens in search of a new nest site, and ant nests tend to cluster. The bad news for the blue grama population is that the queens locate each new nest site in a clump of blue grama. One study at the CPER indicated that ant colony start-ups killed more than sixteen blue grama plants per acre every year.[1] From the point of view of a blue grama plant, a colony of western harvester ants is a good immediate neighbor but dangerous when at a slight distance.

Anthill viewed from ground level on the prairie.

Urban dwellers are known to consider the suburbs bland and indistinguishable. Yet suburban residents readily differentiate neighborhoods near a particular school or commuter route and houses on a cul-de-sac, thoroughfare, or corner lot. Just so, the prairie that may appear uniform to an unobservant human resolves into a rich variety of distinctive habitats to an ant.

More than thirty species of ants parcel up the Fromme Prairie. Some ants prefer north-facing slopes or valley bottoms, others are generalists. Ants of the genera *Lasius* and *Pheidole* locate their nests in the soil at the base of a bunchgrass, excavating their galleries among the grassroots. Members of the genus *Formica* like to nest under small rocks or logs. *Iridomyrmex* and *Manica* might have a crater at the nest entrance; harvester ants enter their nest through a mound.

Examine any given patch of the prairie closely and you will see ants crawling through it. From a distance the prairie looks soft and fuzzy. At close range, ant range, it becomes a spiky landscape. On the hillsides, the dry soil between plants is cracked, crusted on its surface and powdery beneath. As with an old-growth forest with soaring trunks and no undergrowth, the grass stems rise above. The bunchgrasses are sufficiently dense that breezes do not penetrate well to the ground, and the air there is even warmer than that above the plant canopy. Down in the swales it is more like an ant jungle, with dense stems and a layer of matted plant litter an inch or so above the ground. But below this raised litter layer there is still no "duff," and the ants wander across cracked, bare soil. In the driest spots, among the prickly pear and yucca, everything is spiky. Tan, gray, and yellow pebbles lie scattered across the powdery soil, along with an occasional angular piece of milky or rosy quartz. Fallen prickly pear pads and yucca pods slowly decay among piles of dried rabbit turds. Dense, tough little bunches of dried grass cast tiny patches of shade that the ants share with grasshoppers like Psoloessa.

Most ants are omnivorous. They vary their diets between the dead bodies of insects, other invertebrates, and small vertebrates and plant products in the form of nectar or plant sap gained from "milking" aphids and other sap-sucking insects. Many of the ants also harvest seeds. The nest of *Pheidole pilifera coloradoensis* (in Greek, the thrifty, hairy ants of Colorado) excavated under a rock near Psoloessa's overwintering spot was still well stocked with wallflower and goosefoot seeds from the summer before. This ant is a generalist, its colonies spread across Colorado from the shortgrass steppe up to the subalpine forests at 8,500 feet elevation. Other species present on the Fromme Prairie beat even this adaptability. *Lasius niger sitkaensis* (dark, hairy ants) lives up to 12,000 feet high among the plants of the alpine tundra; humans first scientifically described a specimen of this species from Sitka, Alaska. In contrast, species such as *Myrmecocystus melliger mendax* (from Greek and Latin etymological roots, a lying or false ant with a honey bladder) live only on the high plains of Colorado, adapt to the heat and dryness, and gain sustenance gathering "honey" from sap-sucking insects.

The ants also change the resources available to other animals. Darkling beetles use the bare soil surrounding ant nests and prairie dog mounds to raise their temperature in the morning. The beetles then use the shade from adjacent standing vegetation to cool down later in the day. Various species of crickets, roaches, and beetles adapted long ago to living in the ant colonies; and the ants milking their aphids assume all the duties of good shepherds, guarding the aphids and themselves against insect scavengers, thieves, and predators. Like prairie dogs, ants maintain small patches of disturbed soil and vegetation that increase the diversity of the prairie.

Although bears rarely wander the Fromme Prairie, demolishing the delicate intricacy of the ant galleries with a few swipes of their huge paws when they do, many other animals prey on the ants. The ant mound near Psoloessa is a favorite resort of a female shorthorned lizard. The lizard's squat, spiny body is usually seen on the ant horizon early in the morning and toward day's end, waiting patiently near the ant nest for unwary stragglers. At midday the lizard buries herself in the sandy soil to escape the heat. Having come out of winter hibernation and mated in late April, the lizard will now eat ants all summer in preparation for the birth of five to ten young lizards at summer's end.

. . . .

As the spring progresses, the birds that breed and rear young on the prairie settle in for the season. Male western meadowlarks sing vigorously from the tops of tall bushes all across the prairie, their sweet, liquid songs rising and falling in the most melodious sound of spring on the grasslands. Each male throws himself into his song—his brown-and-white striped head thrown back toward his stubby body, his long bill open, and his yellow throat with its black "v" pulsing with sound. The meadowlark up the slope from the prairie dog colony around Psoloessa can sing rather loudly despite a bill bristling with insects. From above, the meadowlark presents speckled brown-and-white wings and back that help him hide from the falcons and hawks that might find him a satisfying meal. But from his own level and below, the meadowlark's bright-yellow throat, breast, and belly form an energetic little bundle of spring sunshine.

Below each lustily singing male, his more discrete mate tends a nest on the ground. A domed structure of grass stems interwoven with the surrounding vegetation covers the nest. From an entrance on the side, a network of narrow trails fans out through the grass. Here the female lays five brown-spotted white eggs that she incubates for two weeks.

The lower, softer notes of the mourning doves sound between the boisterous trills of the meadowlarks. Like the meadowlarks, the rosy-tan and gray doves forage mostly on the ground, but they specialize in the seeds of grasses. Filling its crop quickly with seeds, a dove then settles down to digest the seeds slowly. Fine gravels swallowed to act as grinders aid the digestion of hard seeds. Having migrated to the grasslands in flocks, the doves are also busy raising the first of their multiple broods of the year. The female lays two white eggs in a flimsy platform of twigs built in a shrub. Both parents incubate the eggs for two weeks and then begin feeding the nestlings on pigeon milk. The walls of the dove's crop, an enlarged pocket of the upper esophagus, secrete a milky fluid rich in fat and protein during the nesting season. At the prompting of a young bird inserting its bill into an adult's mouth, the adult regurgitates pigeon milk. Over the course of two weeks the young ones change gradually from a diet of pigeon milk to one of seeds.

A two-spotted skipper butterfly passes over the sunny slope above the nests of the meadowlarks and doves. This rare little butterfly lays its eggs on the sedges growing along the drainage-ways. The caterpillars emerge in midsummer, feed on leaves while living in nests of rolled leaves, then hibernate through the winter. They burst forth the following spring as brown-winged adults with reddish-orange or pale spots. The adults remain near the small channels and wet meadows, feeding on nectar from milkweed and other flowers.

The milkweed is a favorite with many insects, including the monarch butterflies returning from their wintering grounds in Mexico. Millions of monarchs spend the cold months clinging to the trunks of pine trees, sometimes covered by snow. Trusting their frail-looking wings to carry them across thousands of miles of mountains and deserts, generations of monarchs return in summer to lay their eggs on the sappy milkweed plants.

Humans once found uses for milkweed, too. Native Americans sometimes cooked the flowers down into syrup. They used the milky sap to eliminate warts and skin parasites, and the roots produced compounds good for treating ills from constipation to venereal disease, kidney stones, asthma, and cancer. Other parts of the plant served as a contraceptive or a snakebite remedy.

Among the long-distance migrants returning to the prairie to feast on the abundance of spring are yellow warblers that arrived fairly recently, flying at night from wintering grounds in the tropics. Although most warblers nest in trees, a pair of the birds sets up housekeeping in a bush down the slope from the spot where Psoloessa lives, presenting a potential threat to the small grasshopper as they busily pluck insects from twigs and foliage. Each warbler hovers briefly before a plant as it searches and flies out after any insects that take flight; Psoloessa avoids detection by remaining still with her body aligned with the leaves of grass.

The female warbler builds a compact open cup of weed stalks and grass for her nest. She insulates the nest with plant down and animal fur, ready for the four to five greenish-white speckled eggs she incubates for almost two weeks while her mate feeds her. The male sings his bright, sweet song as she flits about after beetles, spiders, mosquitoes, and caterpillars. He is sunshine yellow with streaks of brown along his wings, sides, and breast. His morning song is intended for other warblers, but his most immediate threat is more insidious. A brown-headed cowbird has noted the location of the warblers' nest and is biding its time. These grayish-brown birds lay their eggs in the nests of other birds and then move on. The host birds are left to raise the young cowbirds, usually at the expense of their own hatchlings.

Milkweed in bloom, Fromme Prairie.

Cowbirds originated in the shortgrass prairie, where their parenting technique may have allowed them to follow the herds of bison and other large grazers, feeding on the seeds and insects exposed in the herds' wake. Their nest-stealing technique is very successful. Cowbirds have spread to the tallgrass prairies and eastern woodlands, seriously affecting the nesting success of small songbirds already stressed by habitat loss.

A female cowbird produces eggs as efficiently as a domestic chicken. The cowbird can lay from two to five eggs per week and up to forty eggs a season. Sometimes she lays her eggs with the existing eggs; sometimes she tosses the original eggs out or eats them. Unwilling foster parents raise only a small percentage of the cowbird eggs to maturity, but the percentage is sufficient to steadily increase cowbird numbers over time.

The warblers have a strategy, however. When a cowbird parasitizes a yellow warbler nest, the warbler builds a new floor over the cowbird eggs and lays another clutch of its own eggs. The cowbirds and warblers can renew this cycle repeatedly, with the warbler creating up to six layers in response to five episodes of cowbird parasitism. The warbler's own young leave less than two weeks after hatching, and come August they too join the great night migration back to the tropics.

Among the most conspicuous of the birds nesting on or near the ground on the prairie is the black-billed magpie. Any creature attuned to bird song can hardly miss the loud, sharp cry of this member of the crow family big and bold enough to eat rodents and intimidate housecats. The magpie is strikingly marked. Its black head and bill, iridescent green chest, back, and wings, and white belly and epaulets all streamline into an elegantly long, iridescent green tail. The tail seems to have a life of its own as it bobs swiftly up and down while the rest of the bird voices its displeasure at something. When not vocalizing from the top of a shrub, the male magpie walks along the ground foraging for grasshoppers and caterpillars. A soldier beetle feeding on a goldenrod plant and a large wolf spider scurrying across a patch of bare ground with a load of young spiderlings are equal prey for the magpie, as are the greenish-white eggs on a horned lark nest momentarily left unattended while the parent forages for seeds. Horned larks are uncommon on the Fromme Prairie, but an occasional pair nests in a simple depression lined with grass.

The magpie's nest is a three-feet-wide globular canopy of sticks built in a bush. Inside the stick canopy is a cup-shaped nest of mud lined with grass. Both parents build the nest, where the female sits incubating the six greenish-gray spotted eggs. From her perch on the nest she looks out an entrance hole on either side to observe the latest commotion stirred up by her mate.

* * * * * * * * * * * * * * * *

Psoloessa's days continue to follow a rhythm dictated by the sun. Although air temperatures increase steadily through May, the cool night air can send temperatures as low as 40°F at sunrise. Such cold leaves Psoloessa largely immobile whether she shelters under a bit of plant litter or remains on the soil surface. But she turns her side perpendicular to the source of warmth as soon as the rising sun reaches her patch of ground, basking until the temperature just above the ground reaches 75°F. Psoloessa and other grasshoppers need the sun's warmth, but they have a fairly narrow comfort range; air temperatures a few degrees higher start them moving into shadowed patches, and they actively seek shade when air temperatures rise beyond 90°F. Once in the shade, Psoloessa can assume different postures to further regulate her body temperature, including a straddle position with her hind legs spread away from her body when the air grows really hot. That is not much of a concern until later in the summer, however, and now both nymph and adult grasshoppers remain stationary at night and during much of the day, moving only to eat, mate, and lay eggs. The bigger the grasshopper and the longer its hind legs, the farther it travels in feeding and seeking mates. The larger species move across the microlandscape in a linear fashion, able to leap tall shrubs in a single bound. The smaller species move erratically, carefully detouring around the obstacles presented by a shrub or bunchgrass.

Among the obstacles to grasshopper movement are the local variety of yucca known as soapweed—a spiky plant whose angular outline interrupts the softer shapes of the grasses—and the equally spiky prickly pear. As iconic to the shortgrass prairie as blue grama, the yucca adapted to the drylands by developing rigid, slender sword-shaped leaves that store moisture and minimize its loss. Each grayish-green leaf grows up and out from the base of the plant, creating a cone of sharp edges that discourages casual grazing.

This variety of yucca was widely used by Native Americans. The roots produced suds when rubbed in water and made a nice shampoo. People also used the roots internally to treat digestive irritation and arthritis and externally to reduce hair loss and get rid of body lice. A steamed root poultice formed an anti-inflammatory for bruises, sprains, and bone fractures. The delicately sweet flowers were edible, and the leaves were used for basketry and cordage materials. Immature seed pods were peeled and baked or sliced and dried, and young flower stalks were peeled and steamed.

The name "yucca" was derived from "yuca," a Carib Indian name for the cassava or tapioca plant. Naturalists apparently named the forty species of yucca native to Mexico and the western United States after the yuca because of their edible pods and stalks. The different yucca species include forms as diverse as the Spanish bayonet and the Joshua tree, but they all share a unique relationship with the pronuba moth.

The small, dark pronuba moths spend the winter as larvae in a silken cocoon underground. In spring the larvae emerge as adult moths and mate. The pregnant female moths begin collecting sticky pollen grains from yucca flowers. Each moth forms these grains into a little golden ball as she travels from flower to flower. The pistil of a yucca flower terminates in three lobes around a central opening that leads to a recessed stigma. The yucca can only be pollinated if a mass of pollen is forced down into this opening, a service the female pronuba moth provides. After inserting a single, slender egg into the yucca's ovule chamber, the pronuba pushes her little golden ball of pollen down into the flower. Germinating pollen grains send hundreds of sperm-bearing pollen tubes into the yucca ovary, resulting in the fertilization of the immature seeds inside, some of which provide food for the pronuba larva that grows inside the seed pod. The moth larva hatches inside the yucca ovary during the summer and begins to feed on the maturing seeds but consumes only a small percentage of those within the pod. By late autumn the yucca seed capsules split open, and the moth larva burrows into the soil to construct its winter cocoon. The co-dependence of the yucca and pronuba moth illustrates how species coexist or jointly go extinct. No yucca, no pronuba moth. No pronuba moth, no yucca.

Yucca in bloom, Fromme Prairie.

Sprawling less conspicuously than the spiky yucca among the grasses, clumps of plains prickly pear thrive in the disturbed soil churned up by digging around the prairie dog colony. Like yucca, the prickly pears evolved distinctive traits in response to the stresses

LIFE AMONG THE LEAVES OF GRASS

Prickly pear cactus in bloom, Fromme Prairie.

of the drylands. Widely spreading fibrous roots help the cactus catch whatever moisture falls. Each plant has round, flattened joints known as pads, the lines of pads snaking out in various directions from a central root. These green pads are equivalent to stems. They conduct the plant's photosynthesis, for the leaves have been modified to spines. The larger, rigid, barbed spines keep many animals from eating the prickly pear. The plant's second line of defense is the tiny barbed spines growing in a dense clump at the base of each large spine. The spines also trap a layer of still air next to the pad, reducing moisture loss.

The prickly pears host various eaters despite these irritants. Cattle eat the plant to the ground, although grazing also reduces the abundance of competing grasses and facilitates the spread of prickly pear. Insects frequent the waxy yellow flowers that appear later in the summer, and insects, birds, and rodents eat the juicy pads and purplish-red fruits. Seeds spread by birds germinate rapidly, and individual pads detached from the parent plant take root. Humans also like the taste of the pads and fruit once they are de-spined and peeled.

. . . .

Psoloessa continues to end each day with a period of basking until she crawls under the canopy of grasses for shelter during the night. The cooling air that for her signals the loss of movement, for others signals the start of activity. Darkling beetles snuggled into the plant litter at the base of blue grama clumps wait for twilight to resume feeding on the plant. The beetles spend most of their lives as larvae feeding on plant roots and detritus in the soil until they emerge as flightless adults living mostly in the shrubby areas along stream channels. By night the beetles move among the plant buffet, sampling sedges or threeawns here; thistle, fleabane, or globemallow there; and perhaps a mouthful of sagebrush or rabbitbrush or even prickly pear cactus. Although less than an inch long and unable to fly, the darkling beetles are not really impeded in their movement by the shortgrass plants. To their smaller cousins living on the hillslopes and ridge crests, however, the shortgrass is a veritable thicket. These smaller darkling beetles are spread lightly across the landscape, with less than one beetle per square yard.

As twilight obscures colors and shapes across the prairie, the Gnaphosid spiders emerge from their tubular nets spun under rocks or logs or rolled into leaves. Along with the wolf spiders active during the daylight hours, this is the most numerous group of spiders on the prairie. About half of them are juveniles, but by June adults will dominate the population. By August nearly three dozen species of spiders will be active on the prairie.

Cribellate spiders spread their irregular webs in the tops of small shrubs, under rocks, and in the surface litter. The tighter constructions of the sheet-web weavers stretch between blades of grass, and the funnel-web weavers spin gossamer webs that narrow into a mysterious hole in the ground. Sedentary comb-footed spiders spin irregular snares under rocks for their prey. The more active jumping spiders rely on their good vision to catch prey, as do the crab spiders that are as apt to walk backward or sideways as forward. A single acre of land might contain anywhere from 25 to 10,000 spiders actively preying on a variety of smaller creatures. Unlike similarly sized beetles or nymphal grasshoppers, spiders are not especially challenged by the microterrain of the prairie. Neither bare ground nor a shrub poses much of a problem to a highly mobile spider.

In the air above, common nighthawks pass erratically to and fro on their angular wings. The migrant flocks are newly arrived from their wintering grounds in South America and ready to feast on the insects that populate the prairie air during the warmer months. The speckled birds scoop up insects in their wide-gaping mouths as they fly. From below, their angular outline, black wingtips, and white bars on wings and throat stand out distinctly against the darkening sky. The rush of air over their feathers creates a distinctive roar in the deepening twilight.

Smaller night fliers are abroad as well. The giant cecropia moths, five inches from wingtip to wingtip, are out seeking mates. The caterpillars busily ate the leaves of trees growing along nearby stream channels. Now the wings of the adults—strikingly banded in white, black, gray, and cinnamon brown—flutter softly through the dark night. By autumn, nearly thirty species of moths cross the prairie in their restless search for mates. Some of them pollinate night-blooming flowers. Others, such as the Io moth, do not have mouths and live their brief adult lives only to mate and begin the next generation. Searching for the pheromones wafting from other moths, they flutter above a grassy understory busy with furtive shufflings and skitterings.

• • • • • • • • • • • • • • • •

With each day a few more of the nymphs and adult grasshoppers succumb to other insects, birds, lizards, and rodents, even as new nymphs emerge from the soil to take their place. Once upon a time migratory grasshoppers periodically descended on the prairie in the millions. Ice cores from mountain glaciers high in the Rockies reveal layers with hundreds of little bodies of grasshoppers that succumbed to cold as they flew and hopped across the mountains during mass migrations. These migrations lasted until fairly recently. When Englishwoman Isabella Bird traveled near the Fromme Prairie in 1873, she wrote distastefully of the swarms of locusts on the lower floor of her inn. The great migratory swarms of locusts, far from what biblical tradition encourages us to believe, were not a punishment or a sign of nature run amok. They were an overflowing of abundant life as surely as the flights of passenger pigeons that darkened the skies or the immense herds of bison that shook the ground with their running. But by 1902 the Rocky Mountain grasshopper, or locust, was extinct, perhaps the victim of habitat loss in the riverside areas it preferred. Rates of grasshopper decline accelerated during the twentieth century. By the 1930s grasshoppers were designated as agricultural pests, and chemical warfare against them is now widespread. The remaining species of grasshoppers do not have the locust's migratory swarms, but their populations fluctuate widely from place to place and through time as a result of weather, available habitat, and predation.

Many species of grasshoppers do remain, thanks to the resilience of life. Psoloessa, however, does not live long enough to reproduce. Despite her cryptic coloration and limited movement, a young black-tailed prairie dog exploring the area around her burrow mound comes across Psoloessa while the grasshopper basks in the sun one morning. Although primarily an herbivore, the prairie dog occasionally supplements her diet with a grasshopper. The nutrients Psoloessa had ingested from the blue grama and other plants and incorporated into her own tissue now pass on to the prairie dog.

For every atom lost to the sea, the prairie pulls another out of the decaying rocks. The only certain truth is that its creatures must suck hard, live fast, and die often, lest its losses exceed its gains.

—ALDO LEOPOLD*

The prairie dog is a youngster, one of four born that spring to a mature, two-year-old female *Cynomys ludovicianus*. Early French explorers called the animals *petit chien*, or "little dog." Meriwether Lewis, though aware of this name, referred to them as "barking squirrels" or "burrowing squirrels" in his journal, although other members of his expedition used the phrase "prairie dog."[1] European American naturalists named the prairie dogs *Cynomys*, literally mouse-dog in Greek. The New Latin phrase *ludovician* indicated that the mouse-dog was

* Aldo Leopold, *A Sand County Almanac* (New York: Ballantine Books, 1966), 114.

119

Black-tailed prairie dog at an entrance to its
burrow on the Fromme Prairie.

of Louisiana, as in the Louisiana Purchase the naturalists were busily
describing when they named the species.

The little prairie dog spent her first six weeks underground in a
clean, comfortable nest of dry grass, nursing from her mother and
close female relatives. Weighing only half an ounce at birth, she was
born blind and hairless, but instinct guided her. After six weeks of
nursing, Cynomys developed a fur coat and opened her eyes. She
now weighed more than five ounces. In this dog-eat-dog world the
young one's greatest hazard while nursing is infanticide by an invading male or by one of her nurses. Many female prairie dogs try to kill
the pups of their close kin, even though they might nurse those pups
a couple of weeks later.

Having survived the hazards of her early life, the young Cynomys
begins to explore the extensive underground city that forms her family burrow. The family consists of an adult male, three adult females,

and their offspring. The male dominates the family, followed by adult females, and juveniles at the bottom of the dominance hierarchy. Together they share a burrow with multiple chambers and entrances forming an underground maze over fifty feet long. In its deepest portions the burrow reaches fifteen feet below the surface, well beyond the daily fluctuations of temperature and humidity. Slight differences in elevation among the various entrances to the burrow promote ventilation through the extensive networks of subterranean tunnels. The complexities of the burrow system also provide multiple escape paths in case of danger. Only the week before, a badger dug out one of the deeper burrows but failed to get any of Cynomys's family, which took refuge in other branches of the underground tunnel system.

John Charles Frémont and his men attempted to unearth a prairie dog during their 1843 travels across the plains of eastern Colorado. Frémont wrote in his journals that he and his men "labored ineffectually in the tough clay until dark," and he speculated that "all their little habitations communicate with each other."[2] The Long Expedition had more success in 1820, obtaining two prairie dogs after much exertion and finding them to be "in good condition and well flavored."[3]

By late May Cynomys is ready to venture up to the surface. Soon her brothers will leave the family group, traveling up to three miles as they follow channels or roads across the landscape. The males grow to be nearly a foot long and about a pound and a half in weight, approximately 10 percent heavier than their sisters. They live perhaps five years. Cynomys and her sister will remain at the home burrow, eventually rearing their own pups and generally outliving their brothers by another three years.

The surface is a bright, lively place. Spring is well under way by the time the young Cynomys emerges. Tall stalks of yellow wallflowers and more diminutive reddish-orange globemallow bloom among grasses now fully green. Entire hillslopes flush blue with flax, interrupted only occasionally by the white blossoms of aster and lilac blooms of beardtongue. The calls of meadowlarks and red-winged blackbirds sound like arias above the background chorus of insects.

Cynomys surveys this world from an eminence. The adult prairie dogs push, kick, and pound the soil into a mound at each burrow entrance and carefully clip the surrounding tall plants to create unobstructed views. From this mound the pups can see the burrow entrances of neighboring families, part of a colony of nearly 500 prairie dogs that extends across seventy acres.

Cynomys cannot explore freely across this landscape pocked by hundreds of burrow mounds. Family groups within the colony vigorously defend their individual territories against other dogs. Although a family can extend across the better part of an acre and include nearly thirty individuals, most groups consist of a single breeding adult male, three to four adult females, and several non-breeding yearlings and juveniles. Cynomys has easy access to all the burrows within her own family's territory, particularly now that the tense period of February to April has passed. During this period, when pregnant and lactating females defend their nursery burrows against even their closest relatives, the usual amicability within the family gives way to hostility and frequent confrontations. Mothers have good reason to be on their guard during this time of vulnerability among their offspring. Although almost all adult females in the prairie dog colony breed each spring, only about half actually rear their pups because of the high rate of infanticide. Black-tailed prairie dogs are the only mammals among which lactating females regularly kill the offspring of their close relatives. The killers, which commonly cannibalize the infants, tend to be heavier animals than the victimized mothers, but scientists remain uncertain why prairie dogs engage in this behavior.

Infanticides do not disrupt the social life of the family group for long, however. Cynomys's own mother killed and partially ate her half-sister's pups. Caught in the act, the marauder fought vigorously with her sibling before retreating to her own burrow. The victimized mother lost her aggressiveness within a few days and returned to amicably grooming Cynomys's mother and nursing Cynomys and her siblings.

Cynomys's home colony is small compared with those described by early European American travelers who reached the shortgrass plains. Following the Republican River northeast of the Fromme Prairie in 1843, Frémont wrote of bottomlands entirely occupied with prairie dog villages.[4] In 1901 C. Hart Merriam described a Texas prairie dog colony 150 miles wide and 250 miles long that he estimated to include 400 million animals.[5] Merriam was a pioneering naturalist who headed the U.S. Biological Survey and specialized in studies of small mammals. An early critic of predator control, he correctly predicted that bounties on creatures such as hawks, owls, and weasels would result in greater numbers of mice, insects, and other creatures considered pests by humans. Prairie dogs were among those regarded as pests and were targeted for full-scale eradication campaigns. Since Merriam's time, prairie dog populations have plummeted by 98 percent. The dog towns that once stretched from Canada south to Mexico and from the Rockies east to the tallgrass prairies now occupy less than 10 percent of their historical range. These animals have lived on the western prairies for at least 2 million years and probably evolved here, but they have no defense against poisoning, shooting, destruction of habitat, and death by introduced bubonic plague.

Bubonic plague wipes out a prairie dog town as effectively as it once reduced human populations across Europe and Asia. Plague cleared the prairie dogs out of a town only a few miles from Cynomys's colony in 1963, but one species' catastrophe created another's opportunity. Burrowing owls and cottontail rabbits selected the better burrows in the empty colony and kept them open in the absence of the dogs. The return of prairie dogs as migrating males sought new territories led to numerous fights, but the prairie dogs gradually re-took the territory lost to their species.

Prairie dogs eventually return to a town after an episode of plague if some dogs remain alive in that colony or adjacent colonies. The prairie dogs had a harder time recovering from directed extermination by humans as "pest control" grew more widespread and severe during the twentieth century. The primary threat now is habitat destruction as human communities sprawl across grasslands. The U.S. Fish and Wildlife Department determined in 2000 that black-tailed prairie dogs merited listing as a threatened species under the Endangered Species Act, but no action was taken. Some states continue to target prairie dogs as pests, and some jurisdictions require landowners to eradicate prairie dog colonies.

Range managers also argue about the significance of historical population estimates such as those by Merriam. One group of managers has contended that these observations from 1900 represent unnaturally high numbers because prairie dog populations grew as a result of drought and overgrazing by cattle during the 1880s and 1890s. Another group of managers responded, "If the presence of roughly 23,000,000 cattle around 1900 led to inflated numbers of prairie dogs, what would have prevented prairie dogs from becoming equally numerous in the early and mid-1800s, when 30,000,000 bison inhabited the plains and similar environmental conditions prevailed?"[6]

Where people take notice of them, prairie dogs are still as likely to be reviled as adored. Ranchers traditionally regard prairie dogs as the architects of holes uniquely suited to break the legs of passing cattle and horses or as competitors for plants. Suburban dwellers may regard them as akin to rats, "trash" animals best removed for sanitation and safety. Luckily for the prairie dogs, people increasingly notice the little animals' cute faces and endearing antics and sometimes protest when a new shopping development threatens a dog colony. As environmental awareness grows, people also recognize the importance of prairie dogs in a functioning grassland ecosystem. Merriam would surely approve.

* * * * * * * * * * * * * * * * *

The prairie dog colony on the Fromme Prairie, within which the blue grama had started to sprout in late March and Psoloessa had emerged in early April, spreads across a gentle slope with a southern aspect. A narrow, shallow swale lined with cattail plants runs down the slope, bisecting the colony, and a larger creek drains eastward at the base of the slope. Looking out from her burrow mound, the young Cynomys can see the broadly rounded mounds of other prairie dogs and the more sharply peaked mounds of ant nests rising above the surrounding plants, which are shorter here than on sites not regularly grazed by prairie dogs. In response to grazing by the prairie dogs, clumps of blue grama growing within the colony allocate a higher proportion of tissue and nitrogen to their roots than do plants growing away from the colony, which can afford to put more energy into leaves and reproductive structures.

Like other young of the year, Cynomys has a thinner neck and body than the adults and sleeker golden fur. Fur of a slightly more orange cast covers the adults, whose bodies tend to be closer to the ground and less clearly elevated on legs than those of the young prairie dogs. Many of the adults also look a little threadbare, having begun their semiannual molt from long, thick winter fur to shorter,

Looking downslope toward the creek at the prairie dog colony on the Fromme Prairie. Blue grama forms bunches in the foreground, and forbs grow closer to the prairie dog mounds.

sparser summer fur. The adults start to lose fur on their undersides, then the molting spreads to their upper sides, beginning near their eyes and progressing toward their tails.

During these late May days the adults spend most of the day aboveground and about half their time feeding. Busily eating forbs, grasses, and roots around their burrows, adult prairie dogs are not picky eaters. They alter their eating preferences as the season progresses and new plants become tasty. Any plants remaining close to the burrow have to thrive on disturbance and decreased competition from other plants. For this reason patches of mostly bare ground generally surround the burrows at close range. If the prairie dogs prefer anything, it is grasses. Because the dogs eat the grasses, some prairie dog burrows are surrounded mostly by forbs, non-woody plants that die back to the ground each winter. Across the colony, however, plant species diversity and plant protein content are greater than in adjacent areas. The burrowing of the prairie dogs moves minerals from

Young prairie dogs in spring.

the subsoil closer to the surface, making them more available to shallow-rooted plants. These differences in plants on dog colonies presumably explain why pronghorn antelope and bison find prairie dog colonies so attractive, although antelope and bison no longer graze the Fromme Prairie.

On this sunny day in May, the grasses green rapidly. From the low-lying areas with moist soils switchgrass, champion of the grass-

Prairie dog colony with vegetation cleared around the
burrow entrances at lower left and center of view.

roots, draws on roots nearly twelve feet deep as it sends its slender
seed heads towering three feet into the air. In the surrounding poorly
drained sites the stiff, straw-colored stems of inland saltgrass and the
alkali sacaton grow up from soils whitened with salts. The coarse
blades of prairie cordgrass, edged with tiny points, are getting ready
to break forth into slim, twisting seed heads golden in color. Wherever a disturbance creates an opportunity, invasives establish a roothold; cheat grass and thistle in the drier soils, the broad leaves and
fluffy seed heads of reed canarygrass in moister areas. Unlike an animal shedding its thick winter coat for a cooler summer pelt, the prairie goes from a stubbled winter look to a thick summer luxuriance of
vegetation. For a young prairie dog, the diverse stems and seed heads
form a stand as variegated as the trees in a tropical rain forest.

These leaves of grass are energy conduits. Their slender green
blades link herbivores such as prairie dogs, as well as their predators,

to sources of nutrients in the soil and atmosphere. The prairie dogs move among the smorgasbord of grasses, ingesting with each green mouthful brilliance of sunlight and strength of soil.

Spots of other colors stand out among the green grasses where the early flowers are giving way to later bloomers. The bright yellow heads of dandelions introduced from Eurasia have been blooming over a month, the powder puff of white seeds spreading in the true manner of an invasive species. By May the yellow dandelion blooms are joined by yellow salsify, also from Europe, and by native yellow Thelesperma and bladderpod. White yarrow, rosy-purple milkweed, pink poppy mallow and beeplant, and bluish spiderwort spread an artist's palette of colors across the shortgrass. White blossoms of evening primrose, thin and delicate as tissue paper, appear. Tiny yellow blooms of Nuttall's violet peek out among the grass blades. Wherever the ground is disturbed, the tenacious European bindweed sends its roots and stems swiftly into and around and through, its delicate whitish-pink flowers belying the plant's ability to withstand fire, flood, and drought.

Cynomys makes short forays out from her burrow into this world of rapidly growing plants. If she wanders too close to the marshy areas, a red-winged blackbird might dive aggressively at her, his red epaulets seeming to bristle. Mostly the blackbirds are content to find a cattail stalk from which to issue their hollow, reedy trills. If she wanders too close to the concrete path, Cynomys can attract undue attention from the humans and their dogs walking the path during daylight hours. The prairie dogs are the most charismatic megafauna many humans are likely to see on the prairie.

Cynomys moves toward a bunch of blue grama, but a red-tailed hawk sliding along invisible planes of air, wingtips delicately curved upward, sends her scurrying back to safety. Redtails cannot handle larger adult dogs, but a juvenile like Cynomys still forms a possible meal. Two days earlier, a redtail swooped suddenly downward and killed a juvenile prairie dog in the neighboring family group. Two adult dogs rammed the hawk before it could take off again, surprising the big bird and knocking it off balance, but the redtail nonetheless lifted off with its prey.

Between episodes of eating, all the prairie dogs keep a wary eye out for predators and for hostile interlopers. With their keen eyesight,

Nuttall's violet, one of the early bloomers on the prairie.

prairie dogs recognize various types of intruders by their behavior. Each dog's tail reflects its owner's state. When a contented prairie dog is standing still with its head down to eat or moving in leisurely fashion between burrow entrances, its stubby tail turns slowly like a little crank. When the prairie dog grows mildly alarmed, the tail turns faster or shakes like a little rattlesnake. The greatest alarm produces a sprint toward the nearest burrow mound, a freeze into an alert posture, or an alarm call such as a "jump-yip." Scientists who have patiently studied prairie dogs have documented at least eleven different vocalizations among black-tailed prairie dogs. Each of these vocalizations identifies the speaker and either the conditions of the moment or the behavior that is about to occur. The vocalizations also distinguish different types of threats. Biologist Constantine Slobodchikoff found that prairie dogs have different alarm calls for a human before and after the person shoots a gun.[7]

Cynomys watches her father feed at a neighboring burrow entrance. Feces the size and shape of date pits litter the freshly exposed soil about the entrance. Suddenly Cynomys's father stops eating to stare at another approaching adult male, probably one of the adult or yearling males leaving his own family group at this time of year. The approaching male keeps coming, and the resident male chatters his teeth and flares his tail. He gives a quick jump-yip display, throwing his body upward and back as though trying to induce whiplash. Having not produced the desired result, he makes a bluff charge at the intruder. This briefly sends the other male scurrying. When the intruder again turns aggressively the two prairie dogs close, rolling over and over, jumping, squeaking, and biting in a flurry of furious energy that ends abruptly in a standoff with one prairie dog partway down a burrow entrance and the other bristling on the edge. The partially submerged prairie dog slowly returns to the surface, and each male sniffs the other's back end. Something does not smell right, for the males again fight and chase each other. Back and forth, feinting, charging, rolling, and biting, the males fight for thirty minutes. Finally the aggressor moves away. The pups watching the interaction return to their play. The resident male comes over to the females, sniffing their back ends and touching his face to theirs. The females resume grooming one another, and life at the burrow entrance settles back down.

All around Cynomys the comforting hump-backed shapes of other prairie dogs, brownish or whitish-gold in the sunshine, go about their daily activities. Each dog's dark tail tip, dark eyes, and black nails contrast strikingly with the warm colors of its fur. Cynomys "kisses" other members of her family group when returning after even a few minutes away, touching her mouth to the other dogs' faces. She also plays with her siblings, rolling and chasing them around the burrow entrance mound or simply lying beside them in the warm sunshine. Against the background of bird song and the hum of insects, the prairie dogs give periodic high-pitched yips that keep Cynomys alert but not particularly worried. Then a sharp warning call rings out from a distant burrow. Cynomys looks up to see a golden eagle gliding overhead. She initially flattens her body to the ground, rabbit-like, in a manner the older prairie dogs seldom adopt. As Cynomys dives belowground she nearly collides with a rabbit making the same quick escape. Cynomys misses seeing the eagle take a young prairie dog a couple of hundred yards away from the colony. About half of the

Western cottontail rabbit on the prairie.

young prairie dogs born that year will die before next year's young emerge from their burrows. After landing on the prairie dog, the eagle hops upward in brief flight, lands again, then takes off with steady beats of its large wings. The prairie dog colony resounds with chirps of alarm from all the dogs watching from burrow entrances.

A few days before, the same eagle had taken advantage of the skill of other raptors. A pair of ferruginous hawks had worked in tandem to catch an adult prairie dog, which the larger golden eagle had then taken from one of the hawks. Ferruginous hawks regularly feed on prairie dogs. Managers of the city's natural areas have discovered that prairie dog colonies must be at least fifty acres in size to support a stable population of the raptors and have consequently targeted fifty acres as a minimum size for acquiring and preserving colonies.

Across the mixed and shortgrass prairies, wintering insect populations, rattlesnakes, salamanders, burrowing owls, spiders, and rabbits all share prairie dogs' active or abandoned burrows at some point during the year. Pronghorn antelope preferentially graze on established colonies, and bison seek out recently colonized areas. Densities of rabbit populations are higher on colonies, and because rabbits provide a large proportion of the diet of many predatory mammals and birds, prairie dogs indirectly affect these predators' food supply. Including those who prey on the dogs, from black-footed ferrets and coyotes to ferruginous hawks, golden eagles, and prairie falcons, more than 160 species of vertebrates rely on the dogs at some level for survival. Nine other animals species of the mixed and shortgrass prairie are dependent on prairie dogs for their existence and have consequently declined as prairie dog populations have declined: the black-footed ferret, burrowing owl, mountain plover, ferruginous hawk, golden eagle, swift fox, horned lark, deer mouse, and grasshopper mouse. The prairie dogs themselves move soil and aerate the ground, allowing water to soak more deeply into the soil. Their digging and grazing alter soil chemistry and influence the cycling of nutrients among soil, plants, and animals. They can increase the nitrogen content of soil and plants and change the structure and species composition of the plants growing on their colonies. Scientists studying prairie dogs in Badlands National Park of South Dakota found that exotic plants were only half as abundant on prairie dog colonies as off the colonies. Because of all these effects, ecologists consider prairie dogs one of the highly interactive or keystone species of the prairie.

A literal keystone is a wedge-shaped block at the summit of a stone arch. Without the keystone, the arch cannot distribute weight or strain evenly and will not remain stable. Without a keystone species, an ecosystem begins to collapse as many of the intricate interactions and exchanges among individual organisms and populations are interrupted.

* * * * * * * * * * * * * * * *

Sometime after the attack by the golden eagle, Cynomys and the rabbit cautiously reemerge. The rabbit hops away, and Cynomys resumes her spot on the burrow mound. As she watches the shadow of the circling eagle recede, Cynomys scratches herself vigorously to dislodge a flea. Although largely free of ticks, she is plagued by fleas and lice. Inside, blood protozoa, intestinal parasites, roundworms, spiny-headed worms, and tapeworms all share Cynomys's vigorous body, but she is generally healthy and unbothered by her invisible pests. The fleas are the most dangerous parasite because they carry the plague.

Human plague first appears in historical records during AD 541 to 767, when it spread from southern and central Asia through the Middle East to Europe and northern Africa. Subsequent outbreaks between 1346 and 1841 killed millions of people across Eurasia and northern Africa. During the 1860s plague again spread from China, this time reaching the rest of the world. Plague first reached the United States at San Francisco in 1900 and later at other seaports along the Pacific Rim, from which it became established in native rodent populations.

Plague is caused by the bacterium *Yersinia pestis*, which can be transmitted by infected fleas or direct contact between infected mammals. Scientists identified plague in ground squirrels from California in 1908; by the 1940s the disease had spread across all fifteen states west of the 100th meridian. Plague is devastating to black-tailed prairie dogs, killing 95 to 100 percent of the animals it infects and obliterating entire prairie dog colonies within a single season or less. The speed with which plague spreads among prairie dogs probably reflects the frequent contact between individual prairie dogs, the dense population of colonies, and conditions within prairie dog burrows, which favor the survival and reproduction of fleas. Both types of prairie dog fleas living in Colorado can easily infect other prairie dogs within the first twenty-four hours of feeding on an infected animal.

What remains less clear is how plague can break out and kill large numbers of animals, disappear for a time, and then break out once more. The bacterium might live in the bodies of more resistant species of rodents such as mice and kangaroo rats. However the bacterium survives between outbreaks, such outbreaks continue to occur today. The surrounding humans closely watch Cynomys's colony, fearing it as a potential reservoir of the plague.

The prairie dogs across the colony continue their steady eating as Cynomys wanders about her burrow. Each prairie dog forms a two-humped shape as it supports its weight on its hind legs while bending forward to bring food to its mouth with both front paws. The prairie dog holds its tail up and parallel to its body while eating, then rotates or shakes the tail when moving about. One of the prairie dogs spots a human strolling by on the concrete path bounding the dog colony and gives a resounding jump-yip. All of the surrounding prairie dogs follow like a chorus giving salutes to the sky as each animal throws its head and upper body up and backward. The human, curious, stops to watch. Most of the prairie dogs merely chirp repeatedly at the human while retreating to watch from the burrow mound or entrance, but the closest animal feels more threatened. He holds his ground and scolds the intruder with several minutes of rapid-fire breathy squeaks that resemble those emitted by a plastic squeeze toy. His body shaking with the force of his calls, the prairie dog eventually gives ground and very slowly lowers himself into the burrow entrance.

Small heads peer cautiously over the rim of each mound within a minute after the human passes by. Seeing the danger recede, the prairie dogs reemerge to eat and socialize with each other. Having enjoyed consuming Psoloesssa, Cynomys darts out from her mound in pursuit of another grasshopper. Grabbing the hapless insect with her front paws, Cynomys consumes the juicy body and crunchy exoskeleton, much to the disappointment of a thirteen-lined ground squirrel that had been following the grasshopper.

Cynomys and the squirrel share a common ancestor; fossils indicate that prairie dogs diverged from ground squirrels approximately 2 to 3 million years ago. Unlike the northern grasshopper mice that are particularly abundant in the colonies of black-tailed prairie dogs, most thirteen-lined ground squirrels prefer abandoned prairie dog colonies. The squirrels eat a varied diet of roots, leaves, flowers, and prickly pear fruit, as well as grasshoppers, beetles, ants, and even lizards. Like the prairie dogs, they live in an underground burrow but go into partial hibernation during the winter, remaining belowground and feeding on stored vegetation. Also like the prairie dogs, ground squirrels have a short life expectancy.

Having lost the grasshopper to Cynomys, the squirrel wanders a hundred yards away to a sprawling prickly pear cactus. The lidless eyes of a prairie rattlesnake lying coiled beside the cactus see the squirrel coming, and the snake's sensitive scales and bones detect the

Prairie dog directing alarm calls at a watching human as the prairie dog gradually retreats into its burrow entrance.

vibrations from the little animal's movement. A forked black tongue flicks the air as the snake tastes the wind for scents. This hunting is almost too easy for the snake, with its ultra-sensitive pits between eye and nostril capable of detecting on the darkest night the minute temperature differences caused by a warm mammalian body. The rattler draws its body slowly into a lopsided S-shaped coil. Its subtle markings of cream, brown, and gray might necessitate the hollow, slurred sound of a warning rattle for creatures too large to be prey, but the ground squirrel warrants no such alarm. The snake strikes forward as the squirrel approaches, injecting a lethal dose of venom and then retreating while the poison kills the ground squirrel. Once the squirrel lies immobile, the rattler flexes its jaws widely and takes the squirrel headfirst. Small, recurved teeth in the rattler's upper and lower jaws grip the inert rodent as the snake steadily engulfs it. The squirrel becomes a bulge moving down the snake's long body. Now the rattler can relax and digest, moving only between sun and shadow to keep its body temperature comfortable.

The snake is only two years old, recently emerged from the abandoned prairie dog burrow in which it had spent the winter with several dozen other snakes. With the warmer ground temperatures of spring, the snakes move up from the den to disperse over tens of square miles. The snakes return to the same den in autumn, perhaps finding their way across the landscape by following scent trails. In its wake each snake leaves a molted skin, like a shining, translucent ghost of itself. Perhaps that ghost serves a warning to other prairie dogs and ground squirrels.

The prairie dogs and ground squirrels are part of a large and varied community of small rodents inhabiting the prairie. Fox squirrels encroaching from adjacent urbanized areas with trees nest aboveground, living on a diet of nuts and seeds. Beneath the dense grass matting the shallow swales lies a maze of vole runways. Prairie voles and meadow voles live in surface runways and underground burrows, eating green vegetation and roots. The voles are active day and night throughout the year. They must remain active to feed the steady stream of hungry little mouths. Female voles are ready to breed within three weeks of their own birth. Each female produces up to ten litters a year, with three to six babies in a litter. Coyotes, foxes, badgers, hawks, and owls all do their part to control the population by gobbling every vole on which they can get their paws or talons. The vole populations go through fat and lean times that keep the predators more or less well fed. House mice, deer mice, and grasshopper mice dig their own burrows into the prairie soil, the deer mice drumming their feet on the ground in alarm when confronted by one of the wandering, pugnacious grasshopper mice. Cottontails and black-tailed jackrabbits share the smaller rodents' green food in the summer, moving to a diet of woody vegetation during the winter.

A human can easily walk the perimeter of the Fromme Prairie's 1,082 acres in a day, but the diversity and abundance of the rodents occupying those acres would take more than a lifetime to categorize and understand. The rodents, birds, and predators share the gently rolling terrain between the uplands and Fossil Creek, with the prairie dog colony as the center of their world. The busy prairie dogs aerate the soil through their burrowing, much as earthworms and soil microorganisms do on a smaller scale. As the prairie dogs clip and graze the vegetation, they create zones of disturbance and regulate the cycling of nutrients between the soil and the plants. The colony is a slightly larger-scale biological island, supporting higher numbers of small mammals and terrestrial predators than surrounding areas and a higher density and diversity of bird species.

Among the birds attracted to the dog colony is a pair of burrowing owls attempting to establish their home in a temporarily abandoned burrow at the edge of the colony just beyond Cynomys's home territory. One of the owls stands at the entrance to the burrow as Cynomys's mother approaches. The owl calls loudly, spreads its wings, and fluffs its feathers. The female prairie dog walks back and forth in front of the owl. Both remain in position for nearly fifteen minutes, reconnoitering. Then the prairie dog rushes the owl, which lifts off in flight. The prairie dog inspects the burrow, then returns to her own burrow entrance. Within a few minutes the owl returns, swooping low over the prairie dog and calling raucously. The prairie dog dives into her burrow, and the owl lands at the nearby entrance of its new home.

• • • • • • • • • • • • • • • •

Clouds moving swiftly on winds from the south coalesce above the prairie dog colony, and rain falls just long enough to wet the soil and smear out the mounded soil at burrow entrances. As soon as the rain stops, prairie dogs across the colony work as individuals or small groups to reshape the mound surrounding each entrance. Digging, scraping, pushing, and piling the surrounding soil using their front and rear legs, the prairie dogs finish the task by pounding the soil into place with the points of their noses, sometimes leaving nose prints in the soil as it dries. Up to three feet high, the mounds help prevent flooding of the burrows during the harder summer rains, as well as providing a vantage point for scanning the surroundings.

The setting sun casts long shadows from behind the gradually dissipating clouds. Cynomys and her kin have a plethora of cones in the retinas of their eyes but few rods, limiting their nocturnal vision. Having started feeding aboveground at dawn, the dogs of Cynomys's family begin to settle into their burrows for the night as dusk approaches. Burrows used for sleeping, like those used as nurseries, contain one or two elliptical nest chambers about a foot high and almost two feet long, packed with dry grass. Each dog chooses one among the three or four burrows in which it usually sleeps, but Cynomys lingers a few moments longer at the surface.

The colony Cynomys inhabits is a changeable place. The stability of each family group's boundaries from year to year largely depends on its system of burrows. Adults of both sexes move the periphery of the boundary outward by digging new burrows, unless prevented by adjacent family groups. In any given year, perhaps half of the colony's prairie dogs might be lost to emigration or death, with new pups or invading males taking their places. Life is short for each prairie dog and usually ends in predation. For the prairie, it is important only that the prairie dog colony remain. The thin skin of life across the landscape repairs itself with new young animals replacing those lost to death. Each death is a necessary part of the vital exchange that creates the skin of life, for each death directly fuels other, abundant life.

Cynomys plays out her part in this exchange. Three coyotes moving parallel to one another at an easy lope pass near the prairie dog colony. Occasionally one coyote fans out to check on a promising movement in the grass, then rejoins the others. Somehow, Cynomys misses seeing the approaching predators, and a female coyote takes the young prairie dog by surprise in a quick charge ending in a pounce. The carbon that had made its way through the blue grama, Psoloessa, and Cynomys passes on into the coyote.

HUNTERS OF THE GRASSLANDS

That the prairie is rich is known to the humblest deer-mouse; why the prairie is rich is a question seldom asked in all the still lapse of ages.

—ALDO LEOPOLD*

The young Cynomys is "a red and digestible joy," in the words of the poet Mary Oliver, which the coyote takes quickly.[1] Cynomys forms the latest of several small meals the coyote eats that evening while moving steadily across the darkening prairie. Often the coyote, *Canis latrans*, hunts alone, her mate and the other adult coyotes spread widely across the twelve square miles of their territory. On this evening she rejoins her two hunting partners as the evening breeze ruffling her thick, golden-brown fur brings the sound of frog calls.

---

* Aldo Leopold, *A Sand County Almanac* (New York: Ballantine Books, 1966), 113.

Fromme Prairie wetlands in early summer.

Down in the cattail marsh the nightly serenade of the boreal chorus frog begins. Having spent the day hidden under logs and plant litter, the frogs emerge at dusk to breed. Their passion results in a mass of eggs, most of which feed the western plains garter snake and other species. Once breeding is done, the adults vanish beneath the mud, emerging again the following spring in an annual cycle they might manage to complete five times. For now the peepers sing loudly and move little, averaging only a few feet each day, their inch-long, green-spotted brown bodies blending well into the marsh vegetation and mud.

But not always well enough to escape the garter snakes. These slender reptiles two to three feet long also blend into their surroundings. Only the yellow or orangish-red stripes along the snake's greenish-gray or brown bodies stand out from the vegetation. Having recently emerged from their winter burrows and rock piles, the snakes intently feed their newly active bodies in preparation for the birth of dozens of live young later in the summer.

The entire prairie quickens from its winter rest, each organism busily feeding itself and storing energy to produce or feed its young. Canis gives a short bark to the deepening twilight, and a male from her pack answers from close by. His bark starts a cottontail rabbit, which he chases a short way until Canis relieves him. A third coyote joins them, and they run the rabbit in relays. Moving at bursts nearing forty miles an hour, they overtake the exhausted rabbit. Canis grabs the rabbit in her mouth and kills it with a series of violent shakes. Each coyote might consume more than 150 rabbits a year. The black-tailed jackrabbits sharing the green plants and woody shrubs with the cottontails are born fully furred and ready to hop, but a coyote might still specialize in them and eat 75 or so during the course of a year—or 5,000 voles, 3,000 kangaroo rats, or some combination of rabbits, jackrabbits, voles, and rats. At one denning pair per square mile or more, the coyotes exert a highly efficient check on the rabbit and rodent populations.

The foothills form black silhouettes against a band of paler sky along the western horizon, and the first stars shine overhead. Canis trots back toward her den, pausing to eat a mouthful of grass and to mark her scent posts with urine. The den is set into a well-drained slope above Fossil Creek south of the prairie dog colony of Cynomys and out of sight of the paved trail crossing the prairie. The den had been dug by a red fox. The coyotes enlarged the den a few years ago and have used it ever since during the mating and rearing seasons. Canis and her present mate reared pups here for three years, sharing the den with another coyote family during the first year.

This year Canis has five hungry pups to feed, and she eagerly explores her hunting territory again after her confinement in the den. Earlier in the spring she had spent a large portion of each day resting and sleeping inside the den as the pups grew inside her. A few days before their birth, she lost some of the fur around her abdomen, baring her enlarged mammary glands. She gave birth in the early morning hours one day at the end of April. After eating the placenta and other waste, Canis licked the pups clean and dry and remained with them in the den until early the next morning.

The pups remained incapable of doing much but crawl, whimper, and suckle until their eyes opened about thirteen days after birth. Lying stretched out on her side, Canis suckled the little pups as they rhythmically pushed their forepaws into her on either side of each nipple. It was a relaxing time; sometimes she fell asleep while nursing and the pups fell asleep clinging to a nipple. When changing her position, Canis normally stood and turned in a tight circle before lying down again. With the vulnerable pups beside her, Canis changed position by pivoting on her side without raising any portion of her body except her head.

The pups emerge from the den during daylight hours about three weeks after their birth but remain cautious about wandering more than a few feet from the den entrance. As Canis returns from her dusk foray this evening, she barks to identify herself to the other adults aggressively guarding the den. Like prairie dogs, coyotes use at least eleven different vocal signals for long-distance communication. At close range they more often rely on postures, gestures, and facial expressions similar to those of domestic dogs.

Canis's pups come out to greet her, their roly-poly bodies and big paws tumbling over each other in their eagerness. She licks the pups before spreading her hind legs slightly and assuming a stable standing posture from which to nurse them. Nursing over, she eats their feces as she has done since their birth. As the other hunting adults gradually come in, they turn their narrow, pointed noses to the starry sky and howl together. The howls rise thinly, grow to a rich, full-throated sound, then break down into yaps and barks before rising once more.

The evening howls of the coyotes and the chorus of the boreal frogs are the time signals that the creatures of the dusk and the night are emerging from their burrows and hidden nooks to take over the prairie. Along the edges of the prairie dog towns the burrowing owls take low, short flights. Hovering over the grasses or perched on a taller shrub, they swoop down on an unsuspecting little mammal or snake. The long-legged owls can also run along the ground, clutching insects or lizards in their talons. Having settled in after their annual flight up from Mexico, the small owls prepare to raise their annual brood of owlets.

Canis leaves her den for one more circuit of the prairie. These early evening hours are prime hunting time, and as she trots steadily along she creates a wake of sudden pauses or dives for cover among the house mice, voles, and rabbits. Canis stops abruptly. Ahead and to her left a cottontail rabbit crouches tensely beside a shallow depression lined with grasses and her own belly fur. The depression shelters a litter of five young rabbits born blind and furless and now, at three weeks old, almost ready to strike out on their own. As with the voles, the average cottontail lives less than a year, for the little rabbits run the gauntlet of creeping and flying predators—the same ills to which the voles are heir. Now the mother cottontail explodes away in a burst of zigzagging speed. Canis is not distracted, however, and quickly eats two of the young rabbits while the others flee toward nearby shrubs for shelter. A short shriek from one of them marks a kill by a great-horned owl.

The great-horned owls patrolling the Fromme Prairie by night are powerful and aggressive hunters. They fly out toward the grasslands each evening from their roosts on the cliff ledges and tree branches in the foothills west of the prairie. Finding a suitable perch, they use their superb hearing and vision to detect the presence of the smaller ones, swooping down on silent wings.

For those primarily hunted, the best way to ensure a next generation is to produce many young. For those primarily a hunter, a better strategy is to invest more energy in a few offspring. Once the female owl lays her two or three dull whitish eggs, she incubates them for a month. Both parents feed the young until they are able to fly six weeks later and continue to feed them for several months after that. This requires a lot of rabbit, vole, and mice bodies, as well as the bodies of hawks, snakes, skunks, ground squirrels, geese, ducks, lizards, and insects. Seemingly everything under the size of a housecat that moves is grist for the owl mill. As the brown- and buff-speckled babies grow, their yellow eyes with black pupils take on the keen look of their parents' eyes, and they sprout the feathered tufts that give the species its common name.

The commotion at the rabbit den alerts a red fox, solitary hunter of the night. Like raccoons, red foxes on the Fromme Prairie reflect the proximity of urban areas. On the Central Plains Experimental Range, the endangered swift fox, native of the shortgrass prairie, hunts some of the same animals as the larger red fox. Silent as a shadow, the agile red fox moves swiftly on the toes of his delicate paws. Little escapes the fox's notice. His big, triangular ears move continually, tuning in the subtle sounds of the night's activities. Each waft of air or turn of his head informs the fox's discerning nose of things unseen. Whiskers sensitive as a cat's help pinpoint even the most minute rustling in the undergrowth. Retinas dominated by specialized photoreceptors and backed by a reflective layer provide night vision more than sufficient to detect a cottontail grazing ahead.

His keen senses also help the fox avoid Canis. The coyote turns back toward her den, and the long, lean body of the fox moves with an undulating motion as he lopes away through the clumps of grass. The fox is an opportunistic hunter. As he moves through the grasses, he quickly and casually snaps up insects disturbed by his passage. A tasty bird flushed from its night roost precipitates a skyward leap, for the fox's disproportionately long hind legs can launch him six feet into the air. Approaching a swale, the fox detects a tell-tale stirring beneath the grass. Cocking his head to listen intently, the fox launches himself from ten feet away to pounce on the vole and kill it with a series of quick bites. As he moves back up the slope, the fox sees a cottontail ahead. Although he is already full, the fox stalks the rabbit at a crouch until he gets close enough for the final explosive chase. Sprinting at forty miles an hour, the fox catches and quickly disables the rabbit by biting its hind legs.

The fox does not simply move immune through the landscape, however. He also has to guard against being hunted. The bears, mountain lions, and wolves that can bring swift death to a fox no longer come to the Fromme Prairie. But coyotes have a strong antipathy to foxes, sometimes killing them without bothering to eat the bodies. Owls, hawks, and eagles are all large and powerful enough to hunt a fox, particularly a young one. Distemper, rabies, and mange also take a toll. As with most creatures, the highest mortality in foxes occurs during the first year of life when the young foxes are vulnerable and dispersing from their mother. On the Fromme Prairie this dispersal can be limited by Canis's family, which has no love for foxes.

. . . .

The family of coyotes settles into its den as the other creatures take up their routines of the night. The den extends more than twenty feet back into the hillslope, with two branches. Canis sprawls on her side, the pups nestling against her to nurse again. Her mate lies curled closer to the entrance, his bushy tail wrapped over his nose. During the night the coyotes grunt and twitch in their sleep, changing position and occasionally waking briefly. The adults emerge from the den once more as the sky begins to lighten in the east. They stretch sleep-stiffened limbs and socialize with one another. Renewing the pack's hierarchy, females defer to males with lowered head and forequarters, and pups roll over to expose their vulnerable bellies to adults.

A narrow band of turquoise forms at the eastern horizon. The adults fan out across a landscape with details still lost in shadows. They are quiet, moving purposefully, alert for rabbits and rodents making an early breakfast among the bunchgrass and sagebrush. Each coyote traces a hunting circuit three or four miles long before returning to the den.

Canis follows the windings of Fossil Creek from a terrace above the stream. Although formed in a dry region, this gently flowing landscape is shaped by water. River water carries sediments down from the mountains and spreads them in broad bands and fans. Water rising from seeps and springs cuts little gullies tilted toward the smaller creeks. Rainwater and snowmelt further round the hillslopes, smoothing away sediment from their sharp, river-cut edges and depositing it at the toe of the slopes. The entire landscape resembles a trough folded about the windings of Fossil Creek and tilted toward the east, where the creek joins the Cache la Poudre River, then the South Platte River, the Missouri River, the mighty Mississippi, and eventually the Atlantic Ocean at the Gulf of Mexico.

Humans gave these names to the water pathways to record their own doings and impressions. Marine fossils in the bedrock along its banks accounted for Fossil Creek's name. French Canadian trappers cached gunpowder along the Cache la Poudre River. Other French Canadian explorers named the Platte River for its flatness. Missouri came from a Native American word for "great muddy" and Mississippi from a Native American name for "great river, or father of waters." The Atlantic was named for the mythical island of Atlantis, supposed to lie in the waters west of Mt. Atlas. Mexico came from the Aztec capital named for their war god Mexitli.

Also superimposed on the lineaments of the Fromme Prairie landscape are the lines conceived by humans. A rectangular grid of roads binds the prairie round about like a cage. Curving ridges pop

A creek winds across the prairie, creating small wetlands.

up unexpectedly, contrary to surrounding topography and drainage, where a stock pond bulldozed across a swale left scars. A sinuous concrete trail winds from one hill down across the creek and up the opposite hill. Barbed wire and wooden fences march across the land's contours at the edges of the prairie in a grid as rigid as that of the

Newly built houses bounding the Fromme Prairie to the north.

roads. Houses encroach tightly on three sides with their alien plants and animals. Canis explores the areas around the houses occasionally, seeking the well-fed rabbits grown lazy on a diet of vegetable gardens and bluegrass turf. Fat housecats and little dogs live there, too, but she lives too well on her wild prey to bother much with them.

Fort Collins is one of the fastest-growing cities in the United States, and a new development of large houses is going in along the north side of the prairie. The builders bulldoze the nourishing bunchgrasses. The sagebrush, sacred to Native Americans who used it to physically and spiritually cleanse the body of impurities and bad spirits, is torn up along with the hardy yucca. The fecund topsoil is scraped away. Bindweed races across the bare lots even as the developer lays sprinkler pipes and plants pines and broadleaf trees on the shortgrass prairie. A coat of herbicides pauses the bindweed momentarily, and the developer slaps down a layer of turf grass to hide the stubborn weed. Despite growing public concern about sprawl and loss of open space, Americans continue to live a boomingly expansive lifestyle of more and bigger houses. The huge, boxy houses sell quickly.

Canis makes a wide loop through the new development, searching for any burrowing rodents that might have escaped when the humans gassed the prairie dog burrows. Two cottontails crouch in the newly planted grass, facing each other across the space of a foot. First one and then the other leaps two feet vertically from the crouch so they look like alternating pistons in a machine. Intent on each other, the rabbits miss seeing Canis until too late, and she catches one.

Turning back downslope, Canis flushes a vole from its runway among the thick mat of grass along a moist swale. She hears the little creature below the grass, cocks her head to carefully gauge its progress, crouches, then springs up and across in a sharp pounce that brings her right down onto the vole. The long, coarse brown fur of the voles commonly mats Canis's droppings. Canis continues down the swale to its junction with a larger channel.

The dried cattail stalks still standing from the previous fall rustle as Canis moves among them. The rising sun bleaches the eastern sky golden-white. The nocturnal animals are retiring for the day, and the creatures of sunlight are returning.

Canis continues downstream. Just over two feet high at the shoulder, the slender coyote can easily disappear briefly among the tall cattails and grasses. She flushes a black-tailed jackrabbit from among the grasses at the base of the slope but he escapes her, turning and twisting as he takes twenty feet at a bound at bursts of thirty-five miles an hour.

The little valley of Fossil Creek gradually deepens as Canis progresses downstream. Now the banks at the outside of each bend in the creek cut steeply into the hillslopes, as though the creek is a big cookie cutter. A small grove of cottonwoods clusters about the creek. The lightest of breezes set the leaves to rustling as though whispering among themselves. This trait led many Native American tribes to accord cottonwoods special reverence as creatures particularly sensitive to the presence of the Great Spirit. The cottonwoods' inner bark also sustained people's horses during lean winter times. Frémont felt the cottonwood "deserves to be called the tree of the desert" because of its ability to grow in sandy soils where few other trees could survive, as well as its ability to indicate water to travelers and to provide fuel for campfires and food for grazing animals.[2]

Moving beneath the cottonwoods, Canis disturbs a bullsnake sunning itself near the burrow in which it will deposit its eggs. The belligerent snake coils itself and hisses loudly. The brown spots spread across its thick tan body resemble those of a rattlesnake, and the snake vibrates its tail. But the tail has no rattles and the streamlined head lacks the triangular shape characteristic of a rattler. Canis leaves the four-foot-long snake to menace the small rodents it pursues into their burrows.

Waterfowl busily feed in a small marsh a few yards farther downstream. With the advent of spring they return from their southerly wintering grounds. First come the common goldeneyes and the diving ducks—redheads, ring-necked ducks, and lesser scaup—then the buffleheads and the dabbling ducks; green-winged teal, mallards, northern pintails, cinnamon teal, gadwalls, American wigeons, and, eventually, blue-winged teal and northern shovelers. These birds carry the restlessness of spring. Passing over the prairie on short, swift-beating wings, they stop briefly to feed in the small wetlands. Most of them nest elsewhere, preferring the larger ponds and marshes to the east where decades of gravel mining have thoroughly cratered the floodplain along the Poudre River.

As Canis watches from a discrete distance, a northern shoveler swims steadily back and forth across the shallow pond. The bird swings its broad black bill from side to side as it swims, skimming the water surface to strain out seeds, insects, and small crustaceans. Its coppery brown underbody just shows above the water surface, and its white breast and sides form a striking contrast with the brown water. The black and white wings and tail are neatly folded and the yellow eyes alert in the dark green head. The heavyset bird is a good flier and it takes off abruptly, unsettling the gadwall also foraging on the pond.

Up the slope from the pond, an early-morning birdwatcher perches intently with a pair of binoculars. On this Saturday he has come to enjoy a little of the prairie's calm. Like many other humans, he endures the abrupt tempos of urban life because he carries within him an unspoken belief that there is and always will be a part of the world where he can retreat and find relaxation. In the apparent calm of the prairie a dozen pairs of alert eyes watch him. As he remains carefully still, the gadwall's attention shifts elsewhere, but Canis remains attentive.

The pale brown and whitish gadwall blends into the dried plant stalks around the pond as it steers clear of a great blue heron motionless in the shallows. Like most of the waterfowl, the heron is a visitor here. Periodically it flies upstream from its roosting site in a cottonwood grove along the Poudre River. The heron has a prehistoric look as it flies with long, slow wing beats, its head hunched back onto its shoulders. In the Fromme Prairie wetlands, it has good foraging for small fish, frogs, snakes, insects, rodents, and other birds. Standing unmoving as a statue, the big, gray-bodied bird waits for a fish to swim near. With a rapid thrust of its powerful orange and gray bill, the bird snaps up its meal and swallows it squirming down.

The great blue heron's ability to detect prey is largely visual. Predatory animals tend to have eyes placed forward in their skulls, with overlapping visual fields and the stereoscopic vision necessary to estimate distance. Birds enhance these abilities by having two or three foveas, areas of densely packed photoreceptor cells where the eye forms a particularly sharp image. Humans have one fovea in each eyeball. Most other vertebrates have none, giving them an acuity of vision comparable to what we see peripherally. They may move through a world that would seem indistinct to us, but what they lack in sharp vision they make up for by hearing, smelling, or sensing vibrations we can barely imagine.

Of course, other creatures see a different world. Rabbits, with eyes set on each side of their skulls, see a broader world; imagine being able to look over your shoulder without moving your head. Nocturnal animals have much more light-sensitive eyes, but they see a world without color. Hawks, with eight times the density of photoreceptors found in the human eye, see a clearer world, more sharply focused at longer distances. The compound eyes of a bee detect a world of discrete motions where we see only blurred continuous movement, as though the bee could separate each frame in a movie film. Reality is as complex as each creature is able to perceive it, and the foraging coyote perceives only a fraction of her surroundings.

• • • • • • • • • • • • • • •

Canis trots along the periphery of a prairie dog town, eliciting a series of sharp alarm calls from the prairie dogs. A burrowing owl appears to give her a nod from its burrow entrance as it moves its head up and down to watch her progress. Now that it is the breeding season, the owls remain active and hunt during the day. Canis has interrupted the male owl's preparation for his courtship display. As soon as the coyote passes, the male owl repeatedly flies up, hovers, then descends to his mate on the ground. He brings her insects and small mammals as well, and the pair nibble at each others' bills and preen each others' feathers. The female will lay her eggs in a nest six feet back in the burrow, incubating them for a month while the male feeds her. Once the chicks are born, both parents feed them until they leave the nest by six weeks of age. Although the parents care for their young assiduously, each year finds fewer of the beautiful little cinnamon-brown owls with creamy spots. Their habitat is fast disappearing. As with so many of the grassland birds, owl numbers are in freefall as new housing developments cover over or slice up the fragments of prairie remaining from the agricultural expansions of past decades.

Canis gives her usual greeting bark as she approaches her den. Naturalist Thomas Say named her species *Canis latrans*, barking dog, in 1832.[3] As a member of Stephen Long's 1819–1820 expedition, Say was the first zoologist to travel as far west as the Colorado Rockies, and he described some of the region's most familiar birds, mammals, and reptiles. Those were the days when the barking dogs spread thickly across the prairie. Traveling through the region in the 1840s, European American immigrant Lansford Hastings wrote of seeing several hundred coyotes during a day's travel, many traveling in packs.[4] Wolves displaced coyotes where they chose to, but that still left plenty of territory for the coyotes.

Despite more than a century of attempted extermination by stockmen, coyotes have spread from their original range in western America toward the east. As their natural enemies the wolves and mountain lions falter under human attack, the coyotes adapt themselves to living near humans, surviving campaigns of shooting, poisoning, and trapping directed against them. Other than humans and golden eagles, about the only things that can now make coyotes falter in most of their range are the tiny deadlies: tapeworms ingested from rabbits, roundworm, hookworm, fleas, lice, ticks, and mange. A coyote may live another eight years after reaching sexual maturity at two years, although the dispersal of pups from the natal den is a risky process with high mortality.

The coyotes, so named by the Spanish after the Aztec name "coy-otl," have roamed the plains since the Ice Ages 2 million years ago. They and the wolves probably diverged from a common ancestor between 2 and 3 million years ago. The Great Plains were a very different landscape in those days. Although the grasses and accompanying shrubs were present, the most obvious and dramatic difference was the large grazing animals. Mastodons and mammoths, camels and horses disappeared because of the combined effects of progressive warming and drying of the climate and hunting by prehistoric humans, leaving only the bison from this once diverse collection of large grazers. The European Americans shot the last of the bison present in eastern Colorado in 1897, leaving the smaller pronghorn antelope and mule deer, supplemented by domestic cattle and sheep, as large grazing animals. European Americans also hunted large predators such as the wolf to extinction on the plains. Only the wily and adaptable barking dog persists.

Canis greets the other members of her family and licks the pups to wake them. Licking maintains the bonds between mother and pups and between adult dogs and also cleans urine and feces from the pups. As the pups become more active outside the den, Canis retrieves pups that stray by licking them and encouraging them to follow her back. The pups are now about a month old, and it is time to start weaning them. Canis stands before the pups with her head down, making sounds and motions indicative of retching. The pups approach curiously and she regurgitates partially liquid, partially digested vole, rabbit, and carrion, then briefly nurses the pups. Stretching out on a patch of dusty ground before the den, she watches the pups play with one another and snap at small deerflies. One of the pups' favorite games is to tumble head-over-paws down the slope before the den, then race back up and tumble down again.

Life is good here. The distant rumble of traffic on Taft Hill Road is a sound to which Canis is accustomed. Spring is well under way, the air warm and gentle and filled with bird song. Her pointed ears readily pick out the varied songs of the plain little Brewer's sparrow, the clear music of the vesper sparrow, and the sharp call notes of lark sparrows passing overhead. Canis yawns broadly and stretches out contentedly near the entrance to the den while the pups go in to sleep.

• • • • • • • • • • • • • • • •

The spring winds that periodically blast across the prairie as though determined to uproot even the tenacious blue grama gradually give way to the heat-shimmered stillness of summer. Each morning begins cloudless and serene. The intense sunlight raises the temperature relentlessly, and the short prairie plants provide little shade. By mid-day, muscular thunderheads tower upward in immense pillars that give scale to the broad prairie sky, bringing a cooling purple storm. The afternoon thunderstorms spread across the prairie in short-lived downpours that swell the little creeks with muddy brown water. By dusk the prairie is usually serene once more, the thunderheads blue-black to the west and in the east palest pink with the last rays of the sun. The calls of the mourning doves sound softly in the fading light. The humid air smells green.

The meadowlarks still sing, but now their call is more often a repetitive chirp rather than a generous outpouring of melody. Males and females busily feed their nestlings on insects gleaned as the birds walk along the ground probing the soil with their bills. Beetles, grass-hoppers, crickets, caterpillars, ants, and spiders all fuel the young meadowlarks once they leave the nest after twelve days, still unable to fly. The parents tend the young for another two weeks, then begin raising their second brood of the year.

A few grasshoppers survive from the clutch of eggs that had pro-duced Psoloessa. The adults remain in the same habitat in which they had developed as eggs and nymphs. Food remains plentiful there, even though the first group of host plants has matured and dried. The adult grasshoppers feed increasingly on the now vigorously grow-ing warm season grasses as summer progresses. A few weeks after fledging, the grasshoppers mate. As each male seeking a mate moves toward a female, he rubs his legs over his body, sending out an acous-tical signal recognized only by a female of his species. When close, the male mounts the female, who either accepts or rejects him by emitting a series of ticking sounds as her hind legs kick out and strike the ends of her wings.

The coyote pups grow noticeably. Canis stops eating their feces as they grow hard and black from the presence of regurgitated meat in the pups' diet. She continues to wean them by nursing more briefly and bringing portions of prey back to the den. Now her return elicits food begging as the pups lick her mouth, nip and paw her muzzle, and whine. The pups establish dominance hierarchies as subordinate pups greet their dominant siblings in the same way after separations as brief as thirty seconds. The dominant male of the litter receives more of these greetings than any other pup.

Canis plays with the pups, using exaggerations of hunting behavior as she chases a pup and then misses upon overtaking it. Sometimes she runs at top speed in wide circles around a pup, other times she runs zigzagging away from it. The pups stalk and pounce on each other and initiate play with other adults, rolling onto their backs in passive submission when overtaken by the adult. However tired she might be, the pups often aggressively solicit play from Canis if she lies down. When they grow too annoying she bites them on the muzzle or pins them to the ground with her mouth.

Canis lures the pups away from the den in small steps. She appears briefly and then leaves suddenly so the pups will follow. She regurgitates away from the den area, forcing the pups to come further for food. She shows them prey but does not let go of the food within the den area. She has to repeat these steps many times at progressively greater distances from the den. When she exceeds their comfort zone, the pups rush back to the den between forays. Within two months, however, they begin to accompany her on hunts. Canis starts their hunting by capturing and severely injuring prey, then relinquishing it to the pups. Although the prairie dogs are hard to capture with their communal lookout system, other rodents serve well for this purpose.

The prairie dogs remain the most visible animals on the prairie, although the dogs are most active early in the morning and during late afternoon and early evening. Some of the dogs grow less vigilant where a paved foot trail bisects a dog colony. The prairie dogs on the north side of the trail are so accustomed to humans passing with leashed house dogs that they are easier prey for the coyotes than the prairie dogs on the south side of the trail, which remain wary.

Many prairie dog mounds have freshly excavated soil filled with scents that entice the coyotes. The coyote pups now actively explore their world. The eldest still regularly checks the greasewood bush where he once miraculously found a headless cottontail, but the adult coyotes have not planted any more carcasses there for him to hunt. The pups gradually grow to their adult length of three feet, their tails filling out to more than a foot in length. At this stage, though, their bodies resemble exceptionally long-legged foxes—skinny, with disproportionately large nose and ears.

The coyotes move through a home colored a hundred shades of white, cream, tan, yellow, green, and brown by grasses and shrubs, with a rainbow of flowering forbs strewn among them. Creamy-pink pussytoes cluster together in a low, dense mat on the dry slopes. The blue flax fields give way to bindweed speckled white among the grasses. Yellowish-white flowers rise above the sweet roots of the American licorice, miracle plant the Native Americans used to cure inflammation, allergies, convulsions, bacterial infections, and spasms.

Down in the moist areas, field mint puts forth flowers of pale blue, and purple blooms crown the field milkvetch. The five blue petals of each larkspur flower form a star with arms broadly open to welcome insects to the central sac containing pollen and nectar. Scarlet gilia puts up tall brightly colored stalks, but they are overtopped by the bright yellow spears of flannel mullein, which can climb four or five feet above the ground.

The mullein is a biennial introduced from Europe. Native Americans discovered that its thick leaves, soft as rabbit ears, made good moccasin linings in cold weather. European Americans used it to line their stockings. Both found it useful as a mild sedative for infected lungs and for soothing earaches. Now the mullein spreads among the sprawling, big-spined pads of the plains prickly pear.

The prickly pear has its own flowers, their velvety green centers surrounded by waxy petals in colors from lemon yellow through rusty gold to mango. The yuccas have erupted into spectacular flower candelabra with three-foot-tall stalks of waxy white, bell-shaped blooms. By midsummer fat, thick-skinned pods with a waxy olive-green exterior replace the flowers. Fluffy seed heads of salsify float like Japanese paper lanterns among the grasses.

Mixed native and exotic grasses, Fromme Prairie.

Despite the flowers' bright hues, grasses dominate the appearance of the prairie at midsummer, their pale, fluffy seed heads like taller flowers. Slender stalks of sideoats grama bend over seed heads hanging at even intervals like dew drops from a spider thread. The tiny, yellowish-green seeds of switchgrass fan out in a delicate spray sensitive to the lightest breeze. Three-branching seed heads of big bluestem turn from green to bronze as the summer days lengthen. By late June the grasses lose some of their freshness and take on the look of curing hay, particularly under the midday sun. Under cloudy skies the landscape still looks green, but only the swales remain vividly so. Even in the swales the soil is dry, though, and crusted white with salts beneath its lush jungle of reeds and sedges.

Midsummer is the season of abundant life, filling the senses with sounds, scents, and colors. The chirps of small birds and the buzzing of insects combine to create a constant humming undertone of busy lives. Butterflies form an ever-changing rainbow above the flowers.

Big blue and black pipevine swallowtails migrate into the prairie for the summer. Resident green-veined whites, a smaller white and brown butterfly, emerge from their cocoons in the damp areas along stream courses where the common sulfur butterflies stop to drink. Monarchs flutter brightly among the milkweed. Bees and other insects industriously gather nectar from the myriad plants in bloom. Birds, spiders, and other predators of the pollinators gather the insects. Spider webs lie scattered across the prairie like left-behind wisps of fog or the tiny parachutes of a miniature invading army.

On an exciting day, the pups might find a black-tailed jackrabbit dozing in a bed scratched out in the shade at the base of a mountain mahogany bush. Native Americans once boiled mountain mahogany twigs to make a laxative or to shrink inflamed hemorrhoids or prostrate glands. The jackrabbit simply likes the cover the bush provides. The coyote pups cannot possibly catch such a fleet runner, but one particular jackrabbit has to find another area to rest after the pups stumble onto her on two successive days.

The jackrabbit had given birth earlier in the summer to her second litter of the year. She lost two of the young almost immediately to a badger, another to a golden eagle. The three remaining young ones begin to fend for themselves after a month, although they do not reach adult size for another half a year. The mother jackrabbit is getting old. White hairs as well as black pepper her dark buff fur. A few white hairs even appear on the black tips of her tail and ears. For nearly eight years she has roamed her ten acres of the Fromme Prairie, living primarily on grasses during the growing season and woody shrubs through the winter. More than once her keen eyesight and exceptional speed saved her from a determined predator. When the coyote pups come around, her long ears sensitive as radar warn her well before they are in sight. Thumping the ground with her big hind feet, she bursts from beneath the mahogany taking hops of five to ten feet at a bound. The white underside of her tail flashes in the sunlight. Once she loses the pups, she finds a shady spot on the slope overlooking the cattail marsh and lies down to rest. Sprawled full length on her stomach with her five-inch-long ears folded over her back, she waits until dusk to begin her nightly foraging.

The cattail marsh continues to be a center of activity. The surviving tadpoles of the chorus frogs begin to develop legs and absorb their tails. Dozens of young garter snakes, each only a few inches long, feed their growing bodies on worms and insects and other small fry. Soon they will be joined by newly hatched eastern yellowbelly racers, active hunters who eat anything they can catch.

Along the margins of the marsh, myriad butterfly and moth caterpillars steadily consume the vegetation, storing energy for their miraculous transformation into winged creatures. Different moth species reach maturity as the summer advances. Broad-winged polyphemus moths named for the one-eyed giant of Greek mythology move across the prairie by night on wings beautifully patterned in a mosaic of autumn colors around large eyespots. Caterpillars that fed on cherry leaves are now Io moths with eyespots on their hind wings that resemble bull's eyes with a black center circled by yellow and black rings. Caterpillars that grew fat on evening primroses growing on the drier ridges of the prairie are now whitelined sphinx moths, with narrow wings that whir in flight like those of hummingbirds. Some of the caterpillars and adult insects go to feed the many adult birds starting their second brood of the season or the new fledglings learning to forage for themselves.

A family of raccoons living in one of the large cottonwood trees beside the marsh forages across the prairie at night. The raccoons are omnivores and the bane of other marsh dwellers. Their sensitive forepaws search out the most carefully hidden creatures, and their keen hearing and excellent night vision make them at home in the darkness. In their journeys the raccoons occasionally encounter the other great omnivore of the dark hours: the skunk. The diets of raccoons and skunks largely overlap, but the skunks are less fond of climbing trees or swimming. By July the mother skunk leads her young up from their underground burrow into the upper world for a year of lessons before they leave to be on their own.

This upper world is also the world of owls, hawks, eagles, coyotes, and mountain lions. The greatest defenses of the pretty little black and white skunks are their infamous scent glands. These defenses are used only if the skunk's life is in danger. One of the coyote pups learns a lesson one twilit evening when her path crosses that of a skunk. The pup halts and cocks her ears eagerly. The skunk arches his back and erects his tail and hair, increasing his size and menace just as a housecat does. When the coyote pup does not retreat, the skunk stamps his feet. The inexperienced pup fails to recognize these warning signs and takes a step forward. The skunk dexterously bends into a U-shape with both head and rump facing his aggressor. Two streams of fluid from scent glands just inside the skunk's anus squirt out in a fine spray that travels nearly ten feet. The spray nauseates the pup, burning her eyes and nasal cavities. She retreats in panicked confusion, and the skunk continues on his way.

To a discerning nose, the prairie contains a wealth of scents— moth pheromones wafting on the night air, the urine-scented trail markers of coyote and fox, lingering traces of rattlesnake wanderings, the daily communications and seasonal behaviors of an ant colony, the boundaries of a range staked out by skunk or mountain lion, the urgent chemical messages sent out by a female short-horned lizard or prairie dog or muskrat or mule deer: I am ready to mate, I am ready to mate. Woven through these scents in a tapestry of sound are the calls of the birds, prairie dogs, and coyotes. This is my territory. I am ready to mate. We must move south. Danger. Let the hunt begin. Welcome home. I am ready to mate.

The young coyotes wander happily through this landscape puls- ing with life and activity. Day by day they grow into their powers and learn their capabilities as a top predator. Their parents teach them wariness, for their teeming world is narrowly bounded by the land- scape of humans. The humans leave large footprints on the land—not an earthen den and the subtle but effective scent posts of a coyote but a house of 5,000 square feet surrounded by a yard drenched with noxious chemicals and miles and miles of pavement connecting the houses and yards. No other creatures can safely use the pavement, although scavengers find carrion there and reptiles sometimes use it to warm themselves. For humans locked into their cars, the pavement represents freedom, mobility, and vital connection to the world. For every other creature, the pavement represents a deadly hazard.

One of the young coyotes is too curious and slow while crossing Taft Hill Road one evening. A passing car strikes him. The force of the impact flings his body into the depression beside the road. He dies within a few minutes.

The prairie recycling system begins to dismantle the coyote's body within hours. Flesh, bones, and fur are parceled out among all the hungry creatures yet alive. The big scavengers rend the body first.

Pickup truck passing along Taft Hill Road, which
bisects the western end of the Fromme Prairie.

Raptors, skunks, raccoons, and magpies tear at the flesh over the next
few hours. A turkey vulture summering on the prairie after its flight
from South America leads others of its kind to the body. Beetles and
other insects carry away smaller portions in their own bodies, and
the microbes of decomposition work rapidly. Small rodents scavenge
the bones, chewing on them for their minerals. Even butterflies stop
to pick up nutrients. In little more than a week the young coyote
is largely gone, dispersed through the soil and air of the prairie on
wings and feet and the revolutions of tiny cells. Only the coyote's
skull remains, the eye sockets picked clean by a red-tailed hawk.

ON THE PRAIRIE WINDS

And if Americans are to become really at home in
America it must be through the devotion of many people
to many small, deeply loved places.

—ELIZABETH COATSWORTH*

After picking over the coyote skull, the hawk lifts off on its broad wings. Flapping steadily, it flies toward its nest in the ponderosa pine groves. The nest is braced between two sturdy branches high up in a pine growing beside a small canyon in the foothills, far away from the roads and trails of people. The canopy of the tree protects the nest from direct sunlight and hard rains. Only gentle summer breezes reach here.

---

* Elizabeth Coatsworth, *Maine Memories* (Woodstock, Vt.: Countryman, 1968), 165.

The hawk's nest sat a little to the east last year, in a huge cottonwood along Spring Creek. That was a good spot, with easy access to the many small animals living along the creek. But a pair of great-horned owls forced the red-tailed hawks, *Buteo jamaicensis*, out. The owls ate the young redtail nestlings and then took over the nest. Here in the foothills Buteo is safe from the owls, but it is a longer distance back to the grasslands where she hunts voles, rabbits, and ground squirrels.

Buteo and her mate construct their sturdy new nest together during early March. Selecting sticks up to half an inch in diameter and two feet long, they build up a bulky bowl of sticks more than two feet across. They then use their wings, beaks, feet, and breasts to shape a center depression five inches deep, which they line with grass stems and feathers. The nest complete, Buteo spends several weeks alone perched on the rim before she lays two whitish eggs blotched with brown over a period of three days. Buteo and her mate take turns incubating the eggs for a month, turning the eggs periodically and holding them against the brood patch, an area of the breast that loses its feathers and develops extra blood vessels to transfer heat from the adult's body to the egg. The eggs cool when the adults interrupt incubation to hunt or move about, but the embryos are less sensitive to cold than to heat and the adults do not have to incubate continuously. The embryos increasingly generate their own heat as they develop. Receptors in the brood patch allow the adults to sense the eggs' temperature, so the adults spend less time sitting on them as incubation progresses.

Then the real work begins. Each chick needs many hours to break through its eggshell and emerges weak and helpless. Buteo broods the downy young chicks continuously during their first day out of the egg, shifting position slowly and carefully so as not to trample the chicks. The male hawk takes over feeding of the young and his mate, going out each day for long hours of hunting. He gulps any food he catches, storing it in his crop, a thin-walled bag off the throat. The male begins to feed the chicks on their second day, a slow process as he bites off tiny bits of prey and offers them to the young birds as they pick at his bill. Each chick's head is so large in proportion to the rest of its body that several days pass before the chick can hold its head up for any length of time. Buteo and her mate discard or partially eat feathers, fur, and large bones from the prey; the smaller bones provide calcium for the chicks.

After two weeks the chicks start to stand erect, and their primary and secondary feathers—the main flight feathers—burst their sheaths. Tail feathers emerge shortly thereafter. These outer feathers eventually form a smooth, streamlined surface, light but flexible, that allows adult birds to fly. By three weeks the young birds are steadier on their feet, walking around the nest and taking notice of the surroundings. This behavior is a little risky, as the adults will not rescue young birds that fall or are accidentally thrown from the nest. Within a month the little hawks begin to beat their wings. This strengthens the muscles that will soon lift the birds in flight. The sensitive muscles attached to the walls of each feather's socket that raise, lower, or rotate the feather grow as well. The growing chicks jump up and down while flapping, testing their rapidly growing strength. They stab playfully at each other with their talons and grab sticks from the nest, developing coordination. Eventually they partially feed themselves when the adults bring in small prey. Adult feathers gradually appear on their thighs, belly, and head.

After another week the young birds venture from the nest, hopping and flapping up to nearby branches. Buteo and her mate spend all their time hunting, trying to fill the ravenous stomachs of the young birds that greedily mob their parents at each return and fight with each other over food.

The young birds venture to more distant branches of nearby trees with the passing days. At two months of age they are fully grown and ready to follow their parents to good hunting grounds. Now that the summer is nearing its end, the young hawks have just left the nest, although it will take them another two weeks to become strong fliers.

Buteo spreads her wings and tail and stretches her feet forward as she lands at the nest. As she settles, she begins to preen her feathers. Nearly 3,000 feathers cover Buteo's body, making preening a continual and vitally important chore. Buteo transfers oil from the preen gland under her tail to the feathers as she works through her feathers with her beak. The preen oil keeps her feathers supple, weatherproofs them, and helps prevent the growth of fungi and bacteria. The oil also absorbs vitamin D from sunlight, which Buteo eats along with dirt and parasites as she preens.

Preening also keeps Buteo's feathers arranged. Each feather consists of closely set rows of filaments, or barbs, branching from a hollow rod. Each barb carries two rows of smaller filaments, the barbules, which must be kept aligned for the feather to function properly. Feathers not only allow Buteo to fly but also insulate her and protect her from injury, sunburn, and rainfall. The shades of brown, gold, and tan subtly patterned across Buteo's feathers provide camouflage and promote the displays by which she communicates with other hawks. Each spring, the feathers line her nest. Maintaining her feathers in good condition is critical to Buteo's survival.

Brown and buff feathers pattern Buteo's body, darker above, lighter below. Her distinctive reddish-brown tail indicates that she is among the 10 percent of her species that live long enough to acquire a red tail. Compared to the other types of hawks with which she shares the prairie, she is medium to large in size and powerfully proportioned, with sturdy broad wings that span four feet and a relatively short tail. Her species has proved particularly resilient to the changes associated with humans.

Redtails are generalists that still range from Alaska south to Mexico and from the Atlantic Coast to the fringes of the Pacific. They do well in human-modified habitats and create minimal interference with human interests. Their broad food preferences mean they are not tied to any single species that might be pushed toward extinction by humans. Because the redtails eat primarily small mammalian herbivores or omnivores, they have a relatively low position in food chains. This means they are less affected by poisons such as the pesticide DDT, which humans once broadcast across the environment. The redtails are adaptable in their behavior and tolerant of climatic extremes. Their one point of vulnerability with respect to humans is their fondness for power lines and utility towers. As a grassland species, redtails prefer to survey the surroundings from a high perch and then swoop down on their prey. Power-line corridors and towers look like specially designed redtail habitat, and the birds seek them out. As a result, redtails are the most commonly electrocuted hawks.

Fortunately there are no power-line corridors on the Fromme Prairie. Buteo stops her preening to watch one of her young ones in a nearby tree. The fledgling has already lost much of its playfulness and devoted itself to the serious business of hunting. Hunting requires

Red-tailed hawk held at the Rocky Mountain Raptor Rehabilitation Center near the Fromme Prairie. This bird, which was infected with West Nile Virus, is no longer able to survive in the wild.

considerable skill, and even adults often fail when swooping down on prey. Although the young bird will not develop fully adult plumage for another two years, its present brown and buff markings provide effective camouflage among the lights and shadows in the tree canopy.

Only their own young are allowed to share the two square miles of territory Buteo and her mate defend against other redtails.

The young redtail had made its first kill earlier that day. On the ground, the bird used the cover of bushes along the creek to patiently stalk a mouse rustling through the undergrowth. Having secured the mouse within its strong claws, the hunter guarded it for an hour before ripping off the mouse's head and consuming the little body. Not a particularly elegant kill by hawk standards, but effective nonetheless. Redtails can survive with remarkably little food if times are hard; as little as three and a half ounces per day keeps them going through lean times.

As Buteo watches, the young redtail jabs sharply with its beak at a spot on its side. It is being harassed by blood-sucking fly larvae, but there is little the bird can do. At least these larvae are only nuisances. Blood-sucking simulid flies kill some young redtails.

Buteo watches the young one for a minute, then scans the forest with her sharp eyes. Each eye is almost as large in diameter as a full-grown human's, and her eyes occupy as much space in her head as does her brain. The sides of each eye are notably concave and, with the longer distance between cornea and retina, give the eye a tubular configuration that affords Buteo better vision at long distances. Her vision is so good that at 500 feet up on a clear day, she can see for twenty-seven miles. Her eyes adjust rapidly from distant to close vision, as she needs when hunting, and her binocular vision covers a field of about fifty degrees. She hears well enough to be attracted by the distress cries of animals but relies primarily on her vision when hunting.

A breeze moves upslope among the trees, one of the warm, moist bodies of air that reach the prairie regularly in spring and summer after a long journey across the plains from the Gulf of Mexico. As these air masses flow across the heated landscape they create the updrafts on which Buteo soars for hours. She seldom goes aloft during calm days, but the prairie experiences few calm days. In addition to the strong and nearly constant lateral winds, summer heat creates thermals that allow Buteo to rise with little effort. Air heated at ground level rises in small, rotating cells. Careful maneuvering allows Buteo and other soaring birds to maintain a constant position, rise, or descend among these currents. Buteo soars efficiently because she uses updrafts of air to buoy her body and relies on air moving past her wings to provide lift rather than using forward motion to generate a flow over the wings as in normal flight. When soaring slowly, she spreads her primary feathers to prevent stalling. Each feather acts as a narrow wing, as well as allowing air to slip through and reducing turbulence. Winds of only 10 to 20 miles an hour induce Buteo to soar for hours with relative ease. She seldom soars higher than 100 feet above the ground because the little animals on which she preys do not remain exposed for more than a few seconds and her attack has to be fast. Although Buteo's top speed in flight reaches 35 or 40 miles an hour, when diving from overhead she reaches speeds of 120 miles an hour, plenty fast to surprise a rabbit or a mouse. Having just eaten, Buteo watches the breeze ruffling the limbs of the pines around her.

Moisture has already been wrung out from the summer air moving inland from the Pacific, for this air has been forced up and over the coastal ranges and the broad crests of the Rockies by the time it reaches the eastern slope of the Colorado Front Range. Summer air coming inland from the southwest has crossed the thirsty deserts of northern Mexico, southern California, Arizona, and New Mexico. But air moving inland from the Gulf of Mexico retains some moisture as it crosses the largely level Great Plains. Slight rises and falls of the ground below can set the air mass swirling off into tornadoes or thunderstorms that water the plains of Texas and Kansas. But sufficient moisture remains to create daily thundershowers when the air meets the rock wall that is the eastern front of the Rockies. The air cools as it is forced upward over this topographic obstacle, and the moisture condenses into hard-driven raindrops that briefly swell Fossil Creek and send muddy brown waters spreading across the valley bottoms. Rainfall does not deter Buteo, but her young ones with their still-developing feathers do not venture out from under cover of the trees during rain showers.

By and large, the prairie stays warm and dry. The mean annual temperature of 48°F incorporates the seasonal extremes of 100°F in summer and –15°F during the cold periods of December and January. During any given twenty-four hours the temperature might fluctuate widely as the sun shines on or withdraws from the dry air. Despite the drama of the occasional March blizzard, three-quarters of the moisture reaching the prairie falls between April and September, but this averages only fourteen inches a year.

Buteo lifts off from her nest with slow, measured wing beats. The graceful beauty of her flight represents a culmination of evolution. Her bones are strong but light, and her reproductive organs become almost nonexistent outside the breeding season to reduce her weight. She has a large heart, lungs that efficiently absorb oxygen, and a high body temperature that facilitates rapid consumption of fuel. All these adaptations keep her aloft in winds gentle or strong.

Flying east, Buteo crosses from the Fromme Prairie into housing developments and then mile after mile of agricultural fields. Using eyesight eight times as powerful as that of a human, she scans the dusty fields for rodents. Unfortunately, rodents living in these fields are likely to come with a dose of the agricultural pesticides the little animals accumulate in their bodies. You are what you eat on the prairie, as elsewhere, and now the process has a deadly significance. Although redtails average seven to eight years of life, Buteo might live more than twenty years. If during this period she ingests enough contaminants with her food, some of the contaminants will steadily accumulate in her bones, tissues, and blood. There they impair the functioning of her body, disrupting her thyroid gland and her growth, thinning the shells of the eggs she lays, or binding to her cells in place of estrogen or other hormones. Longevity is not always an advantage.

Finding relatively poor hunting on the plains to the east, Buteo turns back toward the Fromme Prairie. Because Buteo lives year-round on the prairie, she has the advantage of experiencing relatively less contamination. Some of the other raptors with which she shares the grasslands are less lucky. Another hunter of small mammals is the Swainson's hawk. Like redtails, Swainson's are generalists with respect to food, eating ground squirrels, mice, snakes, lizards, small birds, and, later in the summer, grasshoppers and caterpillars. The big bird is even skilled at catching flying insects in the air. Swainson's are more specialized with respect to habitat than redtails, though. Each summer the Swainson's return to the western prairies across a band from Alberta to Nebraska. They build a platform of sticks lined with plants in a tree or large shrub. Feasting on the prairies' summer abundance, the male feeds his mate while she incubates the

Swainson's hawk held at the Rocky Mountain Raptor
Rehabilitation Center near the Fromme Prairie.

two to three eggs she lays. The young remain with the parents until
the cooler weather of autumn sends the hawks south on their great
annual migration to the pampas of Argentina.

Of more than 500 species of migratory birds that breed in North
America, fewer than three dozen fly as far as the pampas. The hawks
that split into pairs for a few months during the breeding season re-
form for migration into flocks of several thousand birds that feed,
roost, and travel together. Like the redtails, the Swainson's are buteos,
soaring hawks with fan-shaped tails. When they travel en masse to
and from Argentina they depend on thermals, rising updrafts of air.
Forming giant swirling masses of hawks known as kettles, the birds
spiral upward within one thermal, then glide from the top of it to the
next thermal. Sliding from thermal to thermal they move southward,
concentrating as though in a giant funnel through Veracruz, Mexico. Half a million of them can pass through Veracruz each autumn,
forming only a portion of the 3 million raptors migrating through
each year.

An undeniable instinct drives the Swainson's 7,000 miles south
each year. The immature birds migrate first, finding their way to a
place they have never been before. The mature adults follow them,

many not even eating en route. They are hungry when they arrive on the pampas, but food is plentiful. Too plentiful, perhaps.

The numbers of Swainson's hawks had already dropped dramatically when pesticides such as DDT were introduced to the United States and Canada. Then in 1995 and 1996 scientists and birdwatchers noticed a further decline in the species. Investigation revealed tens of thousands of dead Swainson's killed by a poison intended to kill grasshoppers, the organophosphate monocrotophos, when it was applied to fields in Argentina. After kicking through bodies of dead hawks piled one on top of another, some with grasshoppers still crammed in their beaks, outraged Argentinians and international observers managed to get monocrotophos banned. There are fewer Swainson's hawks now, but the graceful hawks with the long, tapered wings, dark above and creamy below, still return to the Fromme Prairie to perch on a high point and carefully scan the landscape.

· · · · · · · · · · · · · · · ·

Buteo lands in a cottonwood along Fossil Creek and settles in. Although she spends considerable time soaring, she also sits for hours at a time and watches from her perch for prey and competitors. Returning to the relative safety of the perch after a successful kill, she dissects with her beak the food stored in her crop. The smaller pieces of food then digest in her two-chambered stomach. The first chamber secretes enzymes and hydrochloric acid. The muscular wall of the second chamber grinds the food with rhythmic contractions. Buteo spits out the indigestible bones and hair in a pellet.

Buteo is one of many hunters of the air on the prairie. During summer numerous pairs of raptor eyes watch the grasses of the Fromme Prairie for the stirrings of small mammals, reptiles, and insects. For these smaller creatures, a fleeting shadow might indicate a ferruginous hawk soaring above with its broad wings held in a shallow "V," ready at a moment's notice to dive down on a snake or a young jackrabbit. Death might come in the form of a seemingly small shape that rapidly grows larger as a golden eagle soaring high above dives earthward. The northern harriers and sharp-shinned hawks are stealth fliers, moving low and fast and appearing suddenly over a ridge crest. Prairie falcons hunt this way, too, following a small bird or mammal with speed and agility as it zigzags in panicked escape. The pretty little American kestrels, smallest of the falcons, prefer to hover on rapidly beating wings before pouncing on a grasshopper, an earthworm, or a vole. Buteo comes in like a fighter jet, wings arched sharply above her compact body, her long, pale legs extended downward into the talons that are her main weapons.

Most of these raptors remain on the prairie year-round, although some golden eagles and northern harriers migrate south during the colder months. Of those that do migrate, some funnel through Veracruz with the Swainson's hawks. Even for a species such as the sharp-shinned hawk, which eats daily while on migration, this immense semiannual trek seems likely to be the great hazard of its life. On each journey the birds fly thousands of miles across the hazards of varying terrain, changeable weather, power lines and towers, airplane paths, and hunters' sights. The birds become flying machines, the fat stored during residency burning hour by hour to fuel them on to the distant resting place. If the resting place or places are not there, the birds die. All of that incredible individual effort and thousands of years of evolving in adjustment with climates and terrain and a hundred other species of predator and prey in an intricate ecological web, all of that ends if the birds have no place to rest and rebuild their exhausted bodies, no place to raise the next generation of their species.

Imagine how the United States looks to a migratory bird. Substantial portions of the country are taken up by crops growing in arrow-straight rows or curving in concentric rings around a central-pivot sprinkler or by cities and suburbs ruled along a grid of streets or rounded up into cul-de-sacs. To a migratory bird searching for large expanses of forest or prairie, the United States looks grim.

As a whole, the grassland birds have declined faster, for a longer period, and over a wider area than any other group of bird species. These declines largely reflect the loss of habitat. Including the tallgrass and mixed grass prairies, the grasslands of the Great Plains are the most endangered ecosystem in North America, and this is reflected in the declining numbers of a third of the bird species unique to these grasslands. The urban interface such as that surrounding the Fromme Prairie translates into diminishing returns. Bird surveys, for example, indicate twice as many grassland-nesting songbirds in the interior of a habitat as on the edges. Moreover, the native species in fragmented habitat have reduced opportunities for dispersal and migration, which causes lower genetic diversity. Songbirds' life cycles and food webs can be disrupted in unexpected ways when invasive exotics such as leafy spurge, mullein, and cheat grass choke out the native species.

Consider the complicated cause and effect of cheat grass on the native sage grouse. Cheat grass hitchhiked to North America in grain shipments, spread across the country along railroad lines, then moved inward between the lines, the tenacious grass seeds lodged in animal coats and human clothing. The highly flammable cheat grass spreads as an understory through native sagebrush communities, facilitating repeated range fires that kill off the sagebrush. This in turn stresses the sage grouse, which can live only in habitat with a particular type of plant structure and density.

Ultimately, the fragmented remnants of grassland may be a death trap for many birds if they serve as sinks because housecats eat the fledglings, cowbirds parasitize the nest, and there are not enough grasshoppers or beetles to feed the young ones. A sink consumes birds slowly but inevitably, pushing the population toward dangerously low levels. Smaller, fragmented habitats tend to be sinks for many native species.

For a redtail searching for a nesting site along the Colorado Front Range, the Fromme Prairie forms an island surrounded by degraded habitat low or completely destitute of the nesting grounds and food necessary to sustain the hawk. But it is still a source for many species. On this 1,082-acre island, biologists have identified at least 99 species of birds, 17 species of mammals, and 7 species of reptiles and amphibians, besides the nearly 300 species of plants and unnumbered insects and other invertebrates.

• • • • • • • • • • • • • • • •

The steady shrinking of her world is more apparent to Buteo with each successive year. Just during the past year, developers sliced off a strip along the northern portion of her hunting ground for a new housing subdivision. On her flights to and from the nest at the base of the foothills, Buteo now detours slightly southward to avoid another tract of houses wedged up against the prairie's northwestern bound-

Foxtail barley, Fromme Prairie.

ary. Now, as the breeze she had felt earlier stirs up a brief rain shower over those houses, she lifts off from her perch and glides across the grasslands.

The late afternoon sun casts long shadows as it sinks toward the summit of the foothills. Below the hawk, different colors and textures of vegetation highlight the most subtle contours of the land. Rivers of foxtail barley bleached tan as it goes to seed lie sinuous amid the green swales.

The prairie's coat of grasses has mostly tawny guard hairs now, although the undercoat remains pale green. Green-podded yucca stalks form ragged lines along the ridges. The summer was dry and only milkweed, mullein, and the indefatigable bindweed still bloom. While the neighboring humans constantly watered their lawns, the plant life of the prairie gradually retreated into seed heads or roots. Only the larger swales remain miraculously wet, fed drop by drop through the slow subterranean movement of water that fell weeks before.

Buteo soars over a tributary of Fossil Creek cut into the shale at the base of a hillslope. Down in the stream-cut a mule deer browses the lower branches of the willows growing along the channel. This woody browse is good nourishment for the deer. In her gut live microorganisms capable of producing the enzymes necessary to break down cellulose from the woody plants into glucose and other compounds she can digest.

The deer's trademark large ears move constantly and independently, keeping the animal apprised of activities around her. As Buteo circles, the deer lifts her head to gaze downstream. Something catches her attention, and after a moment she begins to trot upslope. Buteo spots a mountain lion stalking the deer. The lion crouches in the willows, its tail twitching and ears upright as it moves carefully forward. When the lion sees the deer begin to trot, it explodes into a brief chase. The deer immediately responds by stotting. Her powerful legs launch her into bounding leaps eight yards long, all four feet coming down together like pogo sticks and launching her anew in a pace that briefly reaches thirty-five miles an hour. The big cat gives up after a short chase and walks purposefully in the other direction, the set of his ears and tail clearly indicating a lack of concern. He is a large male, nearly eight feet long from his nose to the tip of his tail. He seldom visits the prairie during the day, but the deer had seemed worth a try.

The deer reaches the ridge crest and turns to watch the tawny lion blend gradually into the grasses. Late in the spring she gave birth to two fawns. One of them she has lost to a mountain lion, but the other waits for her farther up the channel. The fawn lost the white spots splattered across its reddish fur within a month. During its early weeks, the fawn saw its mother only at mealtimes for nursing. Now the young deer travels with her, and the mother still acts as lookout and guide.

Buteo continues downstream, gliding easily on the updrafts rising like long, slow sighs from the heated earth below. Once she might have seen pronghorn antelope below, as well as mule deer, but the fleet-footed pronghorn seldom visited any longer. Unlike the deer, which can travel along the wooded foothills, the pronghorn are creatures of the open plains. Bounding along in twenty-foot leaps at speeds of up to sixty miles an hour, the pronghorn can outpace any other animal in the Western Hemisphere. The pronghorn are creatures of superlatives. Active day and night, they can survive temperature ranges of 130°F to –50°F. They can detect movement up to four miles away. When alerted to danger, they flash white rumps visible to other pronghorn at distances of two miles. But unlike deer, they cannot jump fences. A population estimated at many million in the mid-1800s plummeted to about 20,000 by the 1920s.

The pronghorn still live north and northeast of the Fromme Prairie on lands such as the Central Plains Experimental Range (CPER), beyond the steadily encroaching tide of surburbia. On the grasslands stretching from Colorado north into Wyoming the pronghorn exert their own pressure on the shortgrass prairie vegetation, taking small, distinct bites from the flowers, leaves, and stem ends of their favorite fringed sage and scarlet globemallow.

Along with prairie dogs and bison, pronghorn antelope are the primary native herbivore of the shortgrass prairie. People extirpated bison more than a century ago in Colorado, leaving the prairie dogs and antelope to compete with the introduced cows and sheep. Bison feed fairly selectively, eating primarily grasses. The prairie grasses evolved with this pattern of semi-nomadic herds that responded to shifts in grassland plant communities driven by unpredictable patterns of precipitation and fire. The big herds partially controlled the extent of the grasslands as they moved across the landscape, their grazing and defecation influencing the recycling of nutrients through the soil and plants.

Soil fertility generally declines where rainfall exceeds thirty inches a year because the rainwater leaches nutrients downward through the soil. But studies of African grasslands with big grazing animals have shown peak soil nutrient levels when rainfall is thirty-five to forty-five inches a year. This difference occurs because the big herbivores store the nutrients, returning them to the soil surface in their urine and feces. These nutrients provide critical fertilizer for the grasses and, in a tightly woven cycle, the grass fertility in turn dictates where the herbivores graze. On the American grasslands, bison wallows support distinctive plant communities used by other species such as antelope.

The grasslands historically reflected a mosaic of varying disturbance from grazing and fire at large scales and the activities of prairie dogs, pocket gophers, and ants at smaller scales. The species inhabiting a particular portion of prairie reflected this history. A bare-ground area on which a herd of bison had just grazed might be frequented by mountain plovers, McCown's longspurs, and ferruginous hawks. A region that remained undisturbed for years might have a mixed grass and shrub cover frequented by Baird's and Cassin's sparrows. As the habitat at any place changed in response to disturbance or the lack of it, the insect, bird, and mammal species shifted to another place with a more congenial plant community.

This situation changed with the introduction of domestic animals. Domestic cattle produced the greatest changes in eastern Colorado and the vicinity of the Fromme Prairie. Cattle grazing produces a disturbance of greater frequency than the grazing of bison unless the cows are actively managed and moved frequently. Cows also tend to compete more with antelope for forage. As cows settle into a limited area for a long period, their grazing alters vegetative composition and structure. Their hooves compact the soil, changing soil temperature and moisture as they change the soil's ability to absorb precipitation. Twice as much soil can erode from heavily grazed plots in Colorado as from nearby ungrazed or moderately grazed plots. Cows also increase nutrient cycling rates, thereby introducing the potential for greater losses of carbon, nitrogen, and other nutrients from the soil reservoir. Because of their fondness for wet, cool, shaded areas in a hot, dry landscape, cows preferentially graze along streams—removing streamside vegetation, trampling the stream banks, and increasing water temperature, sediment, and nutrient levels.

Open-range grazing of cattle boomed in the western United States from 1865 to the bitter winter of 1886–1887. Heavy cattle deaths that winter, combined with changing settlement patterns in the West, led to fencing and limited movement for cattle. This limited movement in some areas led to intense overgrazing of the grasslands and a concomitant loss of native plant and animal species. In other areas with less intense grazing, the cattle maintain the health of shortgrass prairie plants in the absence of bison, as documented on the CPER.

• • • • • • • • • • • • • • •

Cattle congregating at a spring on the Pawnee National Grassland.
Windmills generating electricity are barely visible in the distance.

As she glides downstream along the creek, Buteo's sharp eyes pick
up a spotted sandpiper hunting for insects and small fish along the
water's edge. The sandpiper darts up to snatch a flying insect out of
the air, and Buteo swoops into a dive. The sandpiper sees her coming
and speeds away low over the water with rapid bursts of shallow wing
beats and short, stiff-winged glides. The little bird is too swift and
agile for the hawk, which flaps upward and settles on top of a bush.
In the hollow below, the sandpiper resumes its foraging, bobbing its
rear half up and down as it walks along searching for crayfish, earthworms, or bits of carrion.

Buteo spots a cottontail further up the creek. She soars lazily
toward the rabbit, which flattens to the ground. Turning to her right,
Buteo uses a low hill to turn back rapidly beyond the rabbit's sight
and dives down onto the rabbit as it resumes feeding. Buteo grabs the
rabbit with her powerful feet, specially designed to kill with strong,
sharp, highly curved talons and to grasp with roughened pads on the
undersides of the toes. She drives the talons of her contracting foot

into the rabbit's neck as she makes contact, killing the rabbit swiftly. A grown rabbit constitutes prey too large for male redtails, which are slightly smaller than females, and even Buteo struggles slightly to carry the rabbit back to a safer spot on a tree branch. There she systematically rips off the rabbit's fur and tears into its flesh, gulping the rabbit in chunks that she stores in her crop.

The sun sets beyond the foothills, and the evening air grows rapidly cooler. Buteo turns back toward her nest as the owls and other night hunters begin to emerge. Having eaten his fill of frogs and crayfish for the day, a river otter still sports along the creek downstream, repeatedly sliding down the earthen cutbank into a shallow pond. Otters are rare on the Fromme Prairie, but this one had moved downslope from a site in the foothills.

On the slope above the otter, a badger emerges for his nightly activities. The badger's heavy, flattened body presents a striking contrast to the otter streamlined from his small ears to the tapering tip of his tail. The stout, short-legged badger looks more like a wrestler, and he has his own uniform in the white stripe that runs from his nose back over the top of his head. His long front claws and strong body make the badger a powerful digger capable of excavating his own underground burrow and of renovating the burrows of ground squirrels and other small mammals in his nightly search for food. He is also a good fighter, and the other hunters out at night give him a wide berth.

Buteo turns her back on the otter and the badger and returns to the foothills as the first stars appear in the sky. Stroking with her powerful wings, she is not conscious of the incomprehensible extent of space above her. Beginning at the ground surface, the troposphere extends upward 5 to 10 miles. Most of the weather systems that control the hawk's daily and seasonal movements form and decay within this lowest layer. Above the troposphere lies the stratosphere, the zone containing most of the ultraviolet-absorbing ozone so critical to the protection of living organisms. At about 30 miles above the Earth's surface the stratosphere gives way to the mesosphere and then, at 50 miles up, to the thermosphere. Cosmic radiation, solar X-rays, and ultraviolet radiation stream through the thermosphere, separating negatively charged electrons from oxygen atoms and nitrogen molecules, leaving behind swaths of color in the form of the aurora borealis and aurora australis. At 300 to 400 miles up, the thermosphere gives way to the exosphere where atoms of oxygen, hydrogen, and helium form an atmosphere so tenuous that the laws describing the relations among pressure, mass, and temperature for gases cease to be valid. Beyond the exosphere lies the magnetosphere, the zone of electrons and protons derived from the solar wind. At about 50,000 miles the Earth's atmosphere probably merges into that of the sun. But the Earth itself is 93 million miles from the sun, in a galaxy trillions of miles broad, in a universe unmeasured.

The red-tailed hawk hangs momentarily suspended between this infinity of space and the measurable but still incomprehensible thickness of rock below her. All the varied and teeming creatures of the prairie live at the meeting of Earth and sky. In this vanishingly thin film of life, every nutrient, every habitat, every process necessary to living organisms occurs. Any presence within that film is as precarious as though balanced on a single strand of spider web. The film of life itself is as delicate and intricate as a web, swiftly torn asunder by catastrophic change from natural processes and human activities. Yet like a spider's web, the film of life is also impressively strong and resilient, seldom completely destroyed though frequently altered and reduced.

Increasingly, the alterations and reductions come from humans, who assume that it is possible to own something as alive as land. Humans possess the land no more than does an earthworm churning the soil, the blue grama creating a small biological island as the prairie dogs create a larger island, or the coyote or red-tailed hawk keeping the numbers of prairie dogs in check. Humans can simply manipulate the landscape more intensively and over larger distances than other species. But this simple distinction makes all the difference. Perhaps because we directly perceive almost nothing of the biochemical processes necessary to sustain our lives and in fact all life, we take them for granted and alter them in ignorance. Whatever the reason, we narrow the margin of survival for species after species, randomly plucking strands from the intricate web of life until it becomes a tattered fragment barely hanging on.

Wolves no longer howl on the Fromme Prairie. Black-footed ferrets no longer pursue prairie dogs along their maze of burrows. Two-spotted skipper butterflies lay their eggs on sedges less frequently.

The ground no longer trembles with the thunder of a bison herd passing through. Many survivors remain—so many that it is difficult to imagine the abundance that has been lost.

Numbers hardly tell the story, but consider the less visible, less charismatic creatures. Up to 4,000 species of invertebrates can be present above the ground in a few square feet of grassland and many times that number belowground. We have not been able to catalog them all, yet we know that like the birds, they suffer from chemical pollution, from competition with non-native species, and from the loss, fragmentation, and steady impoverishment of their habitat. Plants provide another example. There are approximately 7,500 species of plants in the North American grasslands. Fifty-five of these are presently listed as threatened or endangered in the United States, and an additional 700 are candidates for listing. What a holocaust we would consider it if every tenth person in a population were destroyed. Even more striking, these numbers for the grasslands do not refer to individuals but to entire species.

The losses of the grasslands are the shape of things to come, of things that have come. The worldwide rate of extinction leaped from estimates of one species per day in 1980 to one species per hour in 2000. The grasslands together—the steppes, the veld, the pampas, the prairies—form about a quarter of Earth's vegetation. Before human intervention they may have covered nearly half of the Earth's surface. The Fromme Prairie's island of refuge is being steadily eroded by the relentless currents surrounding it.

. . . .

The prairie is an archetypal symbol of the American West: the vast interior barrier between the eastern United States and the coveted lands of the Oregon Territory and the California goldfields. It is enshrined in the imagery of our pioneer heritage: the great wagon trains moving along the Platte River road, the Native Americans hunting bison, the determined sodbusters and picturesque cowboys. How is it that we have so devoured this landscape that it is now largely a memory? Beyond the margin where they can comfortably sustain our crops, we treat the grasslands as we treat the deserts: as wasted lands to be exploited or thoroughly remade. We plant the drylands with unsuitable crops and then abandon them once the soil fertility is exhausted. We sow missile silos across them and strip-mine their minerals. We make little effort to protect them from our cows, our cars, our weeds, or our houses. As a result, we are now reduced to small islands of grass such as the Fromme Prairie or slightly larger islands such as the national grasslands.

Together these islands form a remnant of what was once part of a larger continent. The Fromme Prairie and the other islands are small, but they are also of a size to be noticed, preserved, and emotionally possessed. Perhaps we are more receptive to the importance of preserving large chunks of functioning ecosystems if we come to know and love a smaller place such as the Fromme Prairie.

This place on Earth, so tiny against the vastness of the planet's surface that it appears on only the most local, detailed maps, encompasses everything in the Earth and the heavens. Elements that coalesced to form a planet early in the solar system's evolution condensed and melted, generating magmas that roil upward from deep within the planet to intrude the overlying crust and cool into rock mountains. Wind and water and the acids of plants and soil organisms break down the rock mountains, forming sediments swept downslope under gravity to the plains below. Sedimentation buries clays and sands from ancient oceans, compressing them into other rocks that in turn weather back to the clays and sands forming the layer of soil vital to living creatures on the Fromme Prairie. This soil reflects hundreds of millions of years of geological processes.

Water molecules that fall as rain on the Indian Ocean are swept up into the Great Ocean Conveyor Belt that cycles water between the ocean basins of the Atlantic and the Pacific. The Atlantic Ocean loses more water through evaporation than it gains through precipitation and runoff from the surrounding continents, but the situation is reversed in the Pacific Ocean. These discrepancies set up an enormous conveyor system, with a warm, shallow current moving from the Pacific across the Indian Ocean, south around Africa, and up into the North Atlantic. As the warm surface water flows northward along the eastern coast of North America in the Gulf Stream, some of it is deflected into the Gulf of Mexico. Winds sweeping inland across the Great Plains carry the water molecules from the Gulf toward the Colorado Front Range, where they fall as summer rain on the prairie.

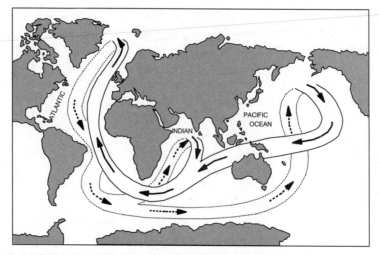

Schematic illustration of the oceanic circulation known as
the Great Ocean Conveyor Belt. Warm surface currents are
indicated by solid lines, cold deep currents by dashed lines.

Streaming down onto the prairie are all the contributions from
the atmosphere. Ultraviolet radiation comes from the distant sun.
Carbon atoms released from cars in Fort Collins by the burning of
fossil fuels mined from deposits of ancient swamps in the deserts
of Saudi Arabia are absorbed by the prairie plants. Nitrogen atoms
that have circulated in the atmosphere for more than a century, since
clearing of a forest to produce fuel for the Industrial Revolution in
Britain released them from storage in the soil, are taken up by soil
microbes.

Frigid air travels down to the prairie from the cold drylands of
the northern pole. Water molecules welling up from the cold, dark
depths of the deep-sea trench off the coast of California evaporate up
into air masses traveling thousands of miles inland across mountains
and deserts, to fall as spring snow on the prairie.

Swainson's hawks fly to the prairie, carrying with them a bit of
Argentina. People come from Africa, to Eurasia, across the Bering
Strait, and down the spine of the Americas to settle here. Or they
come across the Atlantic and then through the eastern woodlands
and the tallgrass prairies, bringing plants that evolved in Eurasia. The

names of the dry grasslands carry the tongues of Utes and Arapaho, Spanish and French.

The prairie also gives forth to the rest of the world, sending water and sediments further downslope in the Mississippi River drainage. The shortgrass steppe exported the cowbird to the eastern United States. It inspired the lyrical words of Mari Sandoz and Willa Cather. The drylands were the source for coyotes moving east and for the prickly pear cacti spreading as weeds across Australia. The prairie sends out its sunshine and nutrients in the tissues of a million birds migrating elsewhere in the world and is a bird source for the surrounding urban and agricultural lands. Wind-blown sediments reaching the prairie from the mountains and the basins to the northwest are stored awhile, then sent on their way further downwind. The liquid melodies of meadowlarks and the scent of fringed sage after rain drift in through suburban windows.

The thin film of life at this tiny place on Earth is at the center of everything. It is Aldo Leopold's round river, a stream of energy flowing from the sun and the atmosphere into the plants and the soil, thence into animals, transformed into nutrients that return to the plants and soil in a never-ending circuit of life. The round river is each point on the Earth and the Earth itself. There are no true islands on this river, no ultimate isolation or withdrawal. There are only differences in the current.

• • • • • • • • • • • • • • •

By autumn the current of the Fromme Prairie slows. The palette of flower colors shrinks as only broom snakeweed and rabbitbrush form clumps of yellow among the green or tan shrubs and grasses. Among the blue grama, the leaves of spring and summer start to die back as the plant contracts its living tissue into the base of stems and roots preparatory to winter dormancy. Purple-brown seed heads of blue grama stand out nearly horizontal from the slender green stems that blend into the surrounding hues of green. Milkweed leaves turn pale yellow along the borders of the marsh, and the leaves of cottonwoods above them form a deeper gold. Piles of dead cattail stalks along the water's edge indicate the high-water mark from a small flood caused by an autumn rain. The remaining grasshoppers

Rabbitbrush blooms in September on the prairie.

become more noticeable as the activity of other insects declines. The ridge crest above the prairie dog colony bristles with dried yucca pods silhouetted against the skyline.

As the Earth tilts its southward pole toward the sun and the nights grow chill, the migrants of summer follow the sunlight to lower latitudes. Some of the sweet-voiced meadowlarks so characteristic of the summer prairie move south to the grasslands of Arizona and New Mexico. Others remain on the prairie but are largely silent. The Swainson's hawks once again undertake their epic journey to the grasslands of Argentina. Adult mockingbirds ignore the adult-sized offspring that follow them closely, persistently screaming to be fed. Buteo scans hills dried to a uniform pale tan, pocked with the little craters of prairie dog mounds. The dogs look scraggly again as their winter fur grows in starting at their tails and progressing toward their eyes and undersides.

On chilly autumn mornings the prairie dogs do not emerge until the sun is well above the eastern horizon. They sit on their hind legs next to the entrance of each burrow, soaking up warmth. On cloudy mornings of damp cold they do not bother to emerge. The prairie dogs shift their feeding from grass stems to seeds and, come winter, to roots and the basal parts of buffalo grass. Each prairie dog moves about slowly, head down, as though gleaning. Periodically the animal scoops at the ground with its front paws and then sits upright on its haunches to hold the plant parts in both front paws as it eats. By November it does not seem possible that the prairie dogs can get any fatter without bursting, yet the heavier animals are more likely to survive the winter and be able to mate and rear numerous offspring.

Black-tailed prairie dogs do not hibernate, but their metabolism slows during the coldest periods. Their periods of torpor grow longer and deeper as temperatures drop during the winter, allowing them to conserve energy. When eating, they seek out plants with more protein and fats because they rely on fatty acids stored in their bodies to

Little bluestem (*left*) and Indian ricegrass (*right*) in autumn, Pawnee National Grassland.

Prairie dog ready for winter.

maintain the low body temperatures of torpor. They can also huddle together to conserve energy; frosty nights of penetrating cold cause all the prairie dogs in a family group to sleep in the same burrow.

The grasses go dormant during October and November. If a plant did not store sufficient carbohydrates during the growing season, the lack of reserves limits its root growth and ability to absorb water and nutrients and can kill the plant before spring. As for many animals, the first year or two of life kills a high percentage of new plants, but mortality rates decline in subsequent years. Blue grama plants that survive the first three years live an average of eight years, and about 5 percent of these survivors live longer than thirty years. Not all of the plants going dormant now will re-green next spring, but the dropping temperatures of autumn trigger the plants to convert stored sugars and starches into more readily available forms as they start to live on their reserves.

Thick, glossy coats cover the deer, and huge racks like branching candelabra balance on the heads of the bucks. Canis and her family now rely more on carrion from dead deer and other large animals rather than hunting the small, widely distributed rodents that make up the bulk of their diet during the rest of the year. The skunks and snakes and others who largely sleep out the cold, dark months settle into their burrows and dens. Arctic air sweeps down from the pole along the spine of the Rockies. When it meets warmer, moister winds blowing eastward from the Pacific, snow comes to the prairie.

The soil dwellers slow or stop their activities as the ground temperature drops. The prairie has subdued days of pale blues and grays and white when the foothills disappear into the clouds and the horizon blurs with snow. Even the occasional chinooks blasting warm air across the prairie fail to thaw the little creeks and marshes for more than a short time. Seeds in the dried yucca pods rattle like castanets. The grasses curl into wispy, golden hay. Each seed stalk of blue grama forms a blonde eyelash above leaves curled into tight little corkscrews. Prairie dog mounds and ant hills dusted with snow stand out strikingly white among the grizzled tan, olive, and brown of the vegetation. Animal trails obscure during the warmer months form irregular lines of white across the landscape. The neatly aligned paw

Small wetland and cottonwood trees in autumn, Fromme Prairie.

Mule deer during autumn in the foothills west of the Fromme Prairie.

prints of fox and the clumped tracks of cottontail crisscross the slopes. Prairie dogs hunched beside their burrows keep an eye on the bald eagle perched in a tall cottonwood. On bitterly cold mornings when sunlight sparkles off the snow crystals, the dog town remains quiet long after the dogs would normally be active. Only the well-tracked paths radiating out from each hole give any sign of habitation. To a raptor or a coyote, the tracks must resemble arrows pointing to food at the central convergence of the hole.

Buteo survives the cold temperatures very well. Her feathers effectively insulate her, and very little skin remains exposed except at feet and bill. She roosts each night in a tree surrounded by enough other trees to provide protection from cold winds. Following the winter solstice, increasing hours of daylight signal her pituitary glands to release hormones that stimulate courtship and ovulation. Male and female reproductive organs increase substantially in size. Buteo and her mate spend more time in the air starting in mid-January. By early February they circle one another in an intricate mating display, each bird rising higher and higher to a thousand feet or more until the male casually moves apart in large loops, dangling his legs as he continues upward. Having gained sufficient height, he folds his wings and swoops down at the female, checking his speed a moment before he hits her and thrusting out his talons so he seems to touch her back before rising abruptly above her again.

Dried seedpods of yucca.

Sparkling mornings when white hoarfrost coats every branch and stem follow nights of thick fog. The whole world becomes crystalline and brittlely white. Even after days of sunshine dry out the rest of the prairie, snow lingers in swales and at the base of north- and east-facing slopes. The prairie dogs remain chubby and well-furred. Flocks of Canada geese make randomly discordant music as they pass

Blue grama on the prairie during winter.

repeatedly back and forth, sensing the urge to migrate yet content to remain here. The winter solstice past, the Earth once more tilts its northern pole toward the sun. The prairie begins to quicken toward a new spring.

NOTES

CHAPTER 1: THE SEA OF GRASS

1. Edwin James, *Account of an Expedition from Pittsburgh to the Rocky Mountains, Performed in the Years 1819 and '20*, 2 vols. (Philadelphia: H. C. Carey and I. Lea, 1823), vol. 1, 418.

2. Bayard Taylor, *Colorado: A Summer Trip* (New York: G. P. Putnam and Son, 1866), 5.

3. Isabella L. Bird, *A Lady's Life in the Rocky Mountains* (Norman: University of Oklahoma Press, 1960), 29.

4. Ibid., 25.

5. Horace Greeley, *An Overland Journey from New York to San Francisco in the Summer of 1859* (Lincoln: University of Nebraska Press, 1999), 99.

6. James, *Account of an Expedition*, vol. 1, 460.

7. Wallace Stegner, *Wolf Willow: A History, a Story, and a Memory of the Last Plains Frontier* (Lincoln: University of Nebraska Press, 1962), 7.

8. Willa Cather, *My Ántonia* (New York: Broadview Literary Texts, 2003), 58.

9. James, *Account of an Expedition*, vol. 1, 138.

10. Cather, *My Ántonia*, 114.

11. Taylor, *Colorado*, 29.

12. William Oliver, *Eight Months in Illinois, with Information to Emigrants* (Newcastle, England: William Andrew Mitchell, 1843), 27.

13. James, *Account of an Expedition*, vol. 1, 473–474.

14. Greeley, *Overland Journey*, 95.

15. Mari Sandoz, *Love Song to the Plains* (Lincoln: University of Nebraska Press, 1961), 2.

CHAPTER 2:
ISLANDS AND ARCHIPELAGOS

1. James, *Account of an Expedition*, vol. 1, 466.

2. John Charles Frémont, *The Expeditions of John Charles Frémont*, vol. 1, *Travels from 1838 to 1844*, ed. D. Jackson and M. L. Spence (Urbana: University of Illinois Press, 1970).

3. James, *Account of an Expedition*, vol. 1, 447.

4. Sandoz, *Love Song to the Plains*, 2.

5. K. F. Dennehy et al., *Water Quality in the South Platte River Basin, Colorado, Nebraska, and Wyoming, 1992–95* (Washington, D.C.: U.S. Geological Survey), 1998.

CHAPTER 4:
LIFE AMONG THE LEAVES OF GRASS

1. D. P. Coffin and W. K. Lauenroth, "Vegetation Associated with Nest Sites of Western Harvester Ants (*Pogonomyrmex occidentalis* Cresson) in a Semiarid Grassland," *American Midland Naturalist* 123 (1990): 226–235.

CHAPTER 5:
KEYSTONE OF THE SHORTGRASS PRAIRIE

1. P. Allen, *History of the Expedition under the Command of Captains Lewis and Clark, to the Sources of the Missouri, thence across the Rocky Mountains and down the River Columbia to the Pacific Ocean* (Philadelphia: Bradford and Inskeep, 1814), vol. 1.

2. John Charles Frémont, *Report of the Exploring Expedition to the Rocky Mountains in the Year 1842 and to Oregon and North California in the Years 1843–44* (Washington, D.C.: Blair and Rives, Printers, 1845), 113.

3. James, *Account of an Expedition*, vol. 1, p. 455.

4. Frémont, *Report of the Exploring Expedition*, 109.

5. C. H. Merriam, *The Prairie Dog of the Great Plains* (Washington, D.C.: USDA Yearbook, 1901).

6. B. J. Miller et al., "Prairie Dogs: An Ecological Review and Current Biopolitics," *Journal of Wildlife Management* 71, no. 8 (2007): 2801–2810 (quote on 2805).

7. Cited in T. T. Williams, *Finding Beauty in a Broken World* (New York: Pantheon Books, 2008).

CHAPTER 6: HUNTERS OF THE GRASSLANDS

1. M. Oliver, *New and Selected Poems* (Boston: Beacon Press, 1992), 54; poem title is "Lonely, White Fields."

2. J. C. Frémont, *The Expeditions of John Charles Frémont*, vol. 1, *Travels from 1838 to 1844*, ed. D. Jackson and M. L. Spence (Urbana: University of Illinois Press, 1970), 442.

3. Cited in James, *Account of an Expedition*.

4. L. W. Hastings, *The Emigrants' Guide to Oregon and California* (Cincinnati, Ohio: George Conclin, 1845).

BIBLIOGRAPHY

ARCHAEOLOGY AND HUMAN HISTORY

Allen, P. *History of the Expedition under the Command of Captains Lewis and Clark, to the Sources of the Missouri, thence across the Rocky Mountains and down the River Columbia to the Pacific Ocean.* Philadelphia: Bradford and Inskeep, 1814.

Bird, I. L. *A Lady's Life in the Rocky Mountains.* Norman: University of Oklahoma Press, 1960.

Cassells, E S. *The Archaeology of Colorado.* Boulder: Johnson Books, 1983.

Cather, W. *My Ántonia.* New York: Broadview Literary Texts, 2003.

Coatsworth, Elizabeth. *Maine Memories.* Woodstock, Vt.: Countryman, 1968.

Debo, A. *A History of the Indians of the United States.* Norman: University of Oklahoma Press, 1970.

Erdrich, L. Big Grass (Northern Tallgrass Prairie, North Dakota). In J. Barbato and L. Weinerman, eds., *Heart of the Land: Essays on Last Great Places.* New York: Pantheon Books, 1994, 149.

Frémont, J. C. *The Expeditions of John Charles Frémont,* vol. 1, *Travels from 1838 to 1844,* ed. D. Jackson and M. L. Spence. Urbana: University of Illinois Press, 1970.

———. *Report of the Exploring Expedition to the Rocky Mountains in the Year 1842 and to Oregon and North California in the Years 1843–44.* Washington, D.C.: Blair and Rives, Printers, 1845.

Greeley, H. *An Overland Journey from New York to San Francisco in the Summer of 1859.* Lincoln: University of Nebraska Press, 1999.

Hastings, L. W. *The Emigrants' Guide to Oregon and California.* Cincinnati, Ohio: George Conclin, 1845.

James, E. *Account of an Expedition from Pittsburgh to the Rocky Mountains, Performed in the Years 1819 and '20,* 2 vols. Philadelphia: H. C. Carey and I. Lea, 1823.

Kalasz, S. M., and C. J. Zier. *The Cass Archaeological Site and Northeastern Colorado Prehistory.* Denver: Colorado Department of Transportation, 1993.

Krech, S. *The Ecological Indian.* New York: W. W. Norton, 1999.

Leopold, A. *A Sand County Almanac.* New York: Ballantine Books, 1966.

Merriam, C. H. *The Prairie Dog of the Great Plains.* Washington, D.C.: USDA Yearbook, 1901.

Norris, K. *Dakota: A Spiritual Biography.* Boston: Houghton Mifflin, 1993.

Noyes, S. *Los Comanches: The Horse People, 1751–1845.* Albuquerque: University of New Mexico Press, 1993.

Oliver, W. *Eight Months in Illinois, with Information to Emigrants.* Newcastle, U.K.: William Andrew Mitchell, 1843.

Sandoz, M. *Love Song to the Plains.* Lincoln: University of Nebraska Press, 1961.

Stegner, W. *Wolf Willow: A History, a Story, and a Memory of the Last Plains Frontier.* Lincoln: University of Nebraska Press, 1962.

Taylor, B. *Colorado: A Summer Trip.* New York: G. P. Putnam and Son, 1866.

West, F. H. The Antiquity of Man in America. In S. C. Porter, ed., *Late-Quaternary Environments of the United States,* vol. 1, *The Late Pleistocene.* Minneapolis: University of Minnesota Press, 1983, 364–382.

Whitman, W. *Leaves of Grass.* New York: Doubleday, 1940.

BIRDS

Austing, G. R. 1964. *The World of the Red-Tailed Hawk.* Philadelphia: J. B. Lippincott, 1964.

Bock, C. E., J. H. Bock, and B. C. Bennett. Songbird Abundance in Grasslands at a Suburban Interface on the Colorado High Plains. In P. D. Vickery and J. R. Herkert, eds., *Ecology and Conservation of Grassland Birds of the Western Hemisphere.* Camarillo, Calif.: Studies in Avian Biology no. 19, Cooper Ornithological Society, 1999, 131–136.

Desmond, M. J., and J. A. Savidge. Satellite Burrow Use by Burrowing Owl Chicks and Its Influence on Nest Fate. In P. D. Vickery and J. R. Herkert, eds., *Ecology and Conservation of Grassland Birds of the Western Hemisphere.* Camarillo, Calif.: Studies in Avian Biology no. 19, Cooper Ornithological Society, 1999, 128–130.

Fowler, D., U. Skiba, and K. J. Hargreaves. Emissions of Nitrous Oxide from Grasslands. In S. C. Jarvis and B. F. Pain, eds., *Gaseous Nitrogen Emissions from Grasslands.* Wallingford, U.K.: CAB International, 1997, 147–164.

Haire, S. L. Spatial Factors Influencing Bird Distribution in Grasslands near Boulder, Colorado. Unpublished MS thesis, Colorado State University, Fort Collins, 1998.

Harness, R. E. Raptor Electrocutions Caused by Rural Electric Distribution Powerlines. Unpublished MS thesis, Colorado State University, Fort Collins, 1997.

Jarvis, S. C. Emission Processes and Their Interactions in Grassland Soils. In S. C. Jarvis and B. F. Pain, eds., *Gaseous Nitrogen Emissions from Grasslands.* Wallingford, U.K.: CAB International, 1997, 1–17.

Johnsgard, P. A. *Prairie Dog Empire: A Saga of the Shortgrass Prairie.* Lincoln: University of Nebraska Press, 2005.

Kaufman, K. *Lives of North American Birds.* Boston: Houghton Mifflin, 1996.

Kingery, H. E. *Colorado Breeding Bird Atlas.* Denver: Colorado Division of Wildlife, 1998.

Knopf, F. L. Conservation of Steppe Birds in North America. In P. D. Goriup, ed., *Ecology and Conservation of Grassland Birds.* Cambridge, U.K.: International Council for Bird Preservation, 1988, 27–41.

———. Avian Assemblages on Altered Grasslands. *Studies in Avian Biology* 15 (1994): 247–257.

———. Prairie Legacies—Birds. In F. B. Samson and F. L. Knopf, eds., *Prairie Conservation: Preserving North America's Most Endangered Ecosystem.* Washington, D.C.: Island Press, 1996, 135–148.

Leslie, D. G. Population Status, Habitat and Nest-Site Characteristics of a Raptor Community in Eastern Colorado. Unpublished MS thesis, Colorado State University, Fort Collins, 1992.

McQuay, P. P. *A Wing in the Door: Life with a Red-Tailed Hawk.* Minneapolis: Milkweed Editions, 2001.

Newton, I. *Population Ecology of Raptors.* Vermillion, S.D.: Buteo Books, 1979.

Peterjohn, B. G., and J. R. Sauer. Population Status of North American Grassland Birds from the North American Breeding Bird Survey, 1966–1996.

In P. D. Vickery and J. R. Herkert, eds., *Ecology and Conservation of Grassland Birds of the Western Hemisphere*. Camarillo, Calif.: Studies in Avian Biology no. 19, Cooper Ornithological Society, 1999, 27–44.

Schmidt, E., and C. E. Bock. Habitat Associations and Population Trends of Two Hawks in an Urbanizing Grassland Region in Colorado. *Landscape Ecology* (2004): 469–478.

Skagen, S. K., A.A.Y. Adams, and R. D. Adams. Nest Survival Related to Patch Size in a Highly Fragmented Shortgrass Prairie Landscape. *Wilson Bulletin* 117 (2005): 23–34.

Snyder, N., and H. Snyder. *Birds of Prey: Natural History and Conservation of North American Raptors*. Stillwater, Minn.: Voyageur, 1991.

Sprunt, A. *North American Birds of Prey*. New York: Harper and Brothers, 1955.

Toombs, T. P. Burrowing Owl Nest-Site Selection in Relation to Soil Texture and Prairie Dog Colony Attributes. Unpublished MS thesis, Colorado State University, Fort Collins, 1997.

Weidensaul, S. *Living on the Wind: Across the Hemisphere with Migratory Birds*. New York: North Point Press, 1999.

Winn, M. *Red-Tails in Love: A Wildlife Drama in Central Park*. New York: Pantheon Books, 1998.

CLIMATE AND PALEOCLIMATE

Berry, J. W.. The Climate of Colorado. In *Climates of the States*, vol. 2. Port Washington, N.Y.: Water Information Center, 1974, 595–600.

Burke, R. M., and P. W. Birkeland. Holocene Glaciation in the Mountain Ranges of the Western United States. In H. E. Wright Jr., ed., *The Holocene*. Minneapolis: University of Minnesota Press, 1983, 3–11.

Forman, S. L., A.F.H. Goetz, and R. H. Yuhas. Large-Scale Stabilized Dunes on the High Plains of Colorado: Understanding the Landscape Responses to Holocene Climates with the Aid of Images from Space. *Geology* 20 (1992): 145–148.

Holliday, V. T. Geoarchaeology and Late Quaternary Geomorphology of the Middle South Platte River, Northeastern Colorado. *Geoarchaeology* 2 (1987): 317–329.

Madole, R. F. Stratigraphic Evidence of Desertification in the West-Central Great Plains within the Past 1000 Years. *Geology* 22 (1994): 483–486.

———. Spatial and Temporal Patterns of Late Quaternary Eolian Deposition, Eastern Colorado, USA. *Quaternary Science Reviews* 14 (1995): 155–177.

Muhs, D. R. Age and Paleoclimatic Significance of Holocene Sand Dunes in Northeastern Colorado. *Annals of the Association of American Geographers* 75 (1985): 566–582.

Osterkamp, W. R., M. M. Fenton, T. C. Gustavson, R. F. Hadley, V. T. Holliday, R. B. Morrison, and T. J. Toy. Great Plains. In W. L. Graf, ed., *Geomorphic Systems of North America*. Boulder: Geological Society of America, 1987, 163–210.

GEOLOGY AND SOILS

Ethridge, F. G. (ed.). *Field Guide, Northern Front Range and Northwest Denver Basin, Colorado*. Boulder: Rocky Mountain Section, Geological Society of America, 1979.

Meldahl, K. H. *Hard Road West: History and Geology along the Gold Rush Trail*. Chicago: University of Chicago Press, 2007.

Ruhe, R. V. Aspects of Holocene Pedology in the United States. In H. E. Wright Jr., ed., *The Holocene*. Minneapolis: University of Minnesota Press, 1983, 12–25.

————. Depositional Environment of Late Wisconsin Loess in the Midcontinental United States. In S. C. Porter, ed., *Late-Quaternary Environments of the United States*, vol. 1, *The Late Pleistocene*. Minneapolis: University of Minnesota Press, 1983, 130–144.

GRASSLAND ECOLOGY

Barrett, J. E. Nitrogen Retention in Semiarid Ecosystems of the United States Central Grasslands Region. Unpublished PhD dissertation, Colorado State University, Fort Collins, 1999.

Bazzaz, F. A., and J.A.D. Parrish. Organization of Grassland Communities. In J. R. Estes, R. J. Tyrl, and J. N. Brunken, eds., *Grasses and Grasslands: Systematics and Ecology*. Norman: University of Oklahoma Press, 1982, 233–254.

Brown, L. *Grasslands*. New York: Alfred A. Knopf, 1985.

Clark, F. E., and R. G. Woodmansee. Nutrient Cycling. In R. T. Coupland, ed., *Natural Grasslands: Introduction and Western Hemisphere*. Amsterdam: Elsevier, 1992, 137–146.

Detling, J. K. Processes Controlling Blue Grama Production on the Shortgrass Prairie. In N. R. French, ed., *Perspectives in Grassland Ecology*. New York: Springer-Verlag, Ecological Studies 32, 1979, 25–42.

Dyer, M. I., J. K. Detling, D. C. Coleman, and D. W. Hilbert. The Role of Herbivores in Grasslands. In J. R. Estes, R. J. Tyrl, and J. N. Brunken, eds., *Grasses and Grasslands: Systematics and Ecology*. Norman: University of Oklahoma Press, 1982, 255–295.

Fahnestock, J. T., D. L. Larson, G. E. Plumb, and J. K. Detling. Effects of Ungulates and Prairie Dogs on Seed Banks and Vegetation in a North American Mixed-Grass Prairie. *Plant Ecology* 167 (2003): 255–268.

Fair, J. L. Demography of Bouteloua Gracilis in Shortgrass Steppe and Mixed-grass Prairie. Unpublished MS thesis, Colorado State University, Fort Collins, 1996.

Fisher, A. G. Seasonal Trends of Root Reserves in Blue Grama and Western Wheatgrass. Unpublished MS thesis, Colorado State University, Fort Collins, 1966.

Flannery, T. *The Eternal Frontier: An Ecological History of North America and Its Peoples.* New York: Atlantic Monthly Press, 2001.

Ford, P. L., and G. R. McPherson. Ecology of Fire in Shortgrass Prairie of the Southern Great Plains. In D. M. Finch, ed., *Ecosystem Disturbance and Wildlife Conservation in Western Grasslands: A Symposium Proceedings.* Fort Collins: USDA Forest Service Rocky Mountain Forest and Range Experiment Station, 1996, 20–39.

Hartnett, D. C., and K. H. Keeler. Population Processes. In A. Joern and K. H. Keeler, eds., *The Changing Prairie: North American Grasslands.* Oxford: Oxford University Press, 1995, 82–99.

Houle, M. *The Prairie Keepers: Secrets of the Grasslands.* New York: Addison-Wesley, 1995.

Johnson, T. Soluble Nitrogen and Phosphorus Fluxes in a Colorado Prairie Marsh. Unpublished MS thesis, Colorado State University, Fort Collins, 1989.

Kelly, R. H. Soil Organic Matter Responses to Variation in Plant Inputs on Shortgrass Steppe. Unpublished MS thesis, Colorado State University, Fort Collins, 1995.

Lane, R. D. Above-ground Net Primary Production across a Precipitation Gradient in the Central Grassland Region. Unpublished MS thesis, Colorado State University, Fort Collins, 1995.

Lauenroth, W. K., and D. G. Milchunas. Short-Grass Steppe. In R. T. Coupland, ed., *Natural Grasslands: Introduction and Western Hemisphere.* Amsterdam: Elsevier, 1992, 183–226.

Lauenroth, W. K., D. G. Milchunas, J. L. Dodd, R. H. Hart, R. K. Heitschmidt, and L. R. Rittenhouse. Effects of Grazing on Ecosystems of the Great Plains. In M. Vavra, W. A. Laycock, and R. D. Pieper, eds., *Ecological Implications of Livestock Herbivory in the West.* Denver: Society for Range Management, 1994, 69–100.

Manning, R. *Grassland: The History, Biology, Politics, and Promise of the American Prairie.* New York: Viking, 1995.

McNaughton, S. J., M. B. Coughenour, and L. L. Wallace. Interactive Processes in Grassland Ecosystems. In J. R. Estes, R. J. Tyrl, and J. N. Brunken, eds., *Grasses and Grasslands: Systematics and Ecology.* Norman: University of Oklahoma Press, 1982, 167–193.

Paruelo, J. M. Regional Patterns and Climatic Controls of the Structure and Function of North American Grasslands and Shrublands. Unpublished PhD dissertation, Colorado State University, Fort Collins, 1995.

Redmann, R. E., and E. G. Reekie. Carbon Balance in Grasses. In J. R. Estes, R. J. Tyrl, and J. N. Brunken, eds., *Grasses and Grasslands: Systematics and Ecology.* Norman: University of Oklahoma Press, 1982, 195–231.

Sala, O. E., and J. M. Paruelo. Ecosystem Services in Grasslands. In G. C. Daily, ed., *Nature's Services: Societal Dependence on Natural Ecosystems.* Washington, D.C.: Island Press, 1997, 237–252.

Savage, C. *Prairie: A Natural History.* Vancouver, B.C.: Greystone Books, 2004.

Seastedt, T. R. Soil Systems and Nutrient Cycles of the North American Prairie. In A. Joern and K. H. Keeler, eds., *The Changing Prairie: North American Grasslands.* Oxford: Oxford University Press, 1995, 82–99.

Schimel, D. S. Nutrient and Organic Matter Dynamics in Grasslands: Effects of Fire and Erosion. Unpublished PhD dissertation, Colorado State University, Fort Collins, 1982.

Scott, J. A., N. R. French, and J. W. Leetham. Patterns of Consumption in Grasslands. In N. R. French, ed., *Perspectives in Grassland Ecology.* New York: Springer-Verlag, Ecological Studies 32, 1979, 89–105.

Scott, N. A. Plant Species Effects on Soil Organic Matter Turnover and Nutrient Release in Forests and Grasslands. Unpublished PhD dissertation, Colorado State University, Fort Collins, 1996.

Sims, P. L., and P. G. Risser. Grasslands. In M. G. Barbour and W. D. Billings, eds., *North American Terrestrial Vegetation,* 2nd ed. Cambridge, U.K.: Cambridge University Press, 2000, 323–356.

Stevenson, F. J. *Humus Chemistry: Genesis, Composition, Reactions.* New York: Wiley-Interscience, 1982.

Stewart, O. C. *Forgotten Fires: Native Americans and the Transient Wilderness.* Norman: University of Oklahoma Press, 2002.

Stolzenburg, W. Town Meeting. *The Nature Conservancy Magazine* July/August (2000): 8–9.

van Andel, J. P., and J. P. van den Bergh. Disturbance of Grasslands: Outline of the Theme. In J. P. van Andel, J. P. Bakker, and R. W. Snaydon, eds., *Disturbance in Grasslands: Causes, Effects and Processes.* Dordrecht: Dr W Junk Publishers, 1987, 3–13.

Wallace, L. L., and M. I. Dyer. Grassland Management: Ecosystem Maintenance and Grazing. In A. Joern and K. H. Keeler, eds., *The Changing Prairie: North American Grasslands.* Oxford: Oxford University Press, 1995, 177–198.

White, R. S., and P. O. Currie. Prescribed Burning in the Northern Great Plains: Yield and Cover Responses of 3 Forage Species in the Mixed Grass Prairie. *Journal of Range Management* 36 (1983): 179–183.

Woodmansee, R. G., and L. S. Wallach. Effects of Fire Regimes on Biogeo-
chemical Cycles. *Ecological Bulletin* 33 (1981): 649–669.

Young, J. A. Historical and Evolutionary Perspective on Grazing of Western
Rangelands. In M. Vavra, W. A. Laycock, and R. D. Pieper, eds., *Eco-
logical Implications of Livestock Herbivory in the West*. Denver: Society for
Range Management, 1994, 1–12.

Zachariassen, J. Ammonia Exchange above Grassland Canopies. Unpublished PhD dissertation, Colorado State University, Fort Collins, 1993.

INSECTS AND INVERTEBRATES

Alba-Lynn, C. Prairie Dogs and Harvester Ants as Disturbance Agents on
the Shortgrass Steppe: Implications for Habitat Heterogeneity. Unpublished MS thesis, Colorado State University, Fort Collins, 2006.

Alba-Lynn, C., and J. K. Detling. Interactive Disturbance Effects of Two Dis-
parate Ecosystem Engineers in North American Shortgrass Steppe. *Oecologia* 157 (2008): 269–278.

Anderson, R. V., C. R. Tracy, and Z. Abramsky. Habitat Selection in Two Species of Short-Horned Grasshoppers. *Oecologia* 38 (1979): 359–374.

Arenz, C. L., and A. Joern. Prairie Legacies—Invertebrates. In F. B. Samson
and F. L. Knopf, eds., *Prairie Conservation: Preserving North America's Most
Endangered Ecosystem*. Washington, D.C.: Island Press, 1996, 91–109.

Bhatnagar, K. N. Growth, Density and Biomass of Grasshoppers in the
Shortgrass and Mixed-Grass Associations. Unpublished PhD dissertation, University of Wyoming, Laramie, 1972.

Capinera, J. L., W. J. Parton, and J. K. Detling. Application of a Grassland
Simulation Model to Grasshopper Pest Management on the North
American Shortgrass Prairie. In W. K. Lauenroth, G. V. Skogerboe, and
M. Flug, eds., *Analysis of Ecological Systems: State-of-the-Art in Ecological
Modelling*. Amsterdam: Elsevier, 1983, 335–343.

Coffin, D. P., and W. K. Lauenroth. Vegetation Associated with Nest Sites of
Western Harvester Ants (*Pogonomyrmex occidentalis* Cresson) in a Semiarid Grassland. *American Midland Naturalist* 123 (1990): 226–235.

Congdon, B. D. Temperature Effects on Development and Fecundity of *Oli-
gonychus pratensis* (*Acari: Tetranychidae*). Unpublished MS thesis, Colorado State University, Fort Collins, 1981.

Detling, J. K., and M. I. Dyer. Evidence for Potential Plant Growth Regula-
tors in Grasshoppers. *Ecology* 62 (1981): 485–488.

Feltwell, J. *The Encyclopedia of Butterflies*. New York: Prentice-Hall General
Reference, 1993.

Gregg, R. E. *The Ants of Colorado*. Boulder: University Press of Colorado,
1963.

Guertin, D. S. Trade-offs between Feeding and Reproduction in a Ball-Rolling Dung Beetle, *Canthon Pilularius (L.)*. Unpublished PhD dissertation, Colorado State University, Fort Collins, 1993.

Hilbert, D. W., and J. A. Logan. A Simulation Model of the Migratory Grasshopper (*Melanoplus sanguinipes*). In W. K. Lauenroth, G. V. Skogerboe, and M. Flug, eds., *Analysis of Ecological Systems: State-of-the-Art in Ecological Modelling*. Amsterdam: Elsevier, 1983, 323–332.

McIntyre, N. E. Landscape Heterogeneity at Multiple Scales: Effects on Movement Patterns and Habitat Selection of Eleodid Beetles. Unpublished PhD dissertation, Colorado State University, Fort Collins, 1998.

Melman, J. Naturally Occurring Feeding Deterrents Effective against Migratory Grasshopper, *Melanoplus sanguinipes (F.)*. Unpublished MS thesis, Colorado State University, Fort Collins, 1982.

Mitchell, J. E., and R. E. Pfadt. A Role of Grasshoppers in a Shortgrass Prairie Ecosystem. *Environmental Entomology* 3 (1974): 358–360.

Myers, P. *Class Oligochaeta (Earthworms)*. University of Michigan, 1996. http://animaldiversity.ummz.umich.edu/annelida/oligochaeta (accessed September 10, 2008).

Russell, R. Density and Taxonomic Composition of Grasshoppers (*Orthoptera: Acrididae*) on and off Black-Tailed Prairie Dog Towns in Mixed Grass Prairie. Unpublished MS thesis, Colorado State University, Fort Collins, 1999.

Russell, R. E., and J. K. Detling. Grasshoppers (*Orthoptera: Acrididae*) and Black-Tailed Prairie Dogs (Sciuridae: *Cynomys ludovicianus* (Ord)): Associations between Two Rangeland Herbivores. *Journal of the Kansas Entomological Society* 76 (2003): 578–587.

Skinner, K. M. Spatial and Multivariate Analyses of Colorado Rangeland Grasshopper Abundances: Pattern and Process. Unpublished PhD dissertation, Colorado State University, Fort Collins, 1999.

Stanford, R. E., and P. A. Opler. *Atlas of Western USA Butterflies*. Denver: Private printing, 1993.

Struttmann, J. M. *Two-Spotted Skipper (Euphyes bimacula)*. U.S. Geological Survey, 1999. http://www.npwrc.usgs.gov/resources/distr/lepid/bfly-usa (accessed April 12, 2008).

Thompson, D. C. Distributional Properties and Optimal Sampling of Shortgrass Rangeland Grasshoppers. Unpublished PhD dissertation, Colorado State University, Fort Collins, 1988.

Ueckert, D. N. Diets of Grasshoppers in Northeastern Colorado. Unpublished PhD dissertation, Colorado State University, Fort Collins, 1969.

Weeks, R. D., Jr. Ground-Dwelling Spiders (*Arachnida: Araneae*) on Shortgrass Steppe in Northeastern Colorado. Unpublished MS thesis, Colorado State University, Fort Collins, 1997.

Welch, J. L., R. Redak, and B. C. Kondratieff. Effect of Cattle Grazing on the Density and Species of Grasshoppers (*Orthoptera: Acrididae*) of the Central Plains Experimental Range, Colorado: A Reassessment after Two Decades. *Journal of the Kansas Entomological Society* 64 (1991): 337–343.

With, K. A. The Translation of Patterns across Scales: Analysis of Movement Patterns in a Grassland Mosaic. Unpublished PhD dissertation, Colorado State University, Fort Collins, 1993.

————. Ontogenetic Shifts in How Grasshoppers Interact with Landscape Structure: An Analysis of Movement Patterns. *Functional Ecology* 8 (1994): 477–485.

Yount, V. A. Diets of Selected Insects in a Grassland Ecosystem. Unpublished MS thesis, Colorado State University, Fort Collins, 1971.

MAMMALS

Armstrong, D. M. *Distribution of Mammals in Colorado*. Monograph of the Museum of Natural History, no. 3, University of Kansas, Lawrence, 1972.

Bailey, V. *The Prairie Ground Squirrels or Spermophiles of the Mississippi Valley*. Washington, D.C.: USDA Division of Ornithology and Mammalogy Bulletin, no. 4, 1893.

Benedict, R. A., P. W. Freeman, and H. H. Genoways. Prairie Legacies—Mammals. In F. B. Samson and F. L. Knopf, eds., *Prairie Conservation: Preserving North America's Most Endangered Ecosystem*. Washington, D.C.: Island Press, 1996, 149–166.

Brizuela, M. A. Prairie Dog Feeding Behavior: Response to Colonization History and Fire. Unpublished PhD dissertation, Colorado State University, Fort Collins, 1987.

Bueler, L. E. *Wild Dogs of the World*. New York: Stein and Day, 1973.

Colby, C. B. *Wild Dogs*. New York: Duell, Sloan, and Pearce, 1965.

Fox, R., and R. Espinosa. *Procyon Lotor: Raccoon*. University of Michigan, 2000. http://animaldiversity.ummz.umich.edu/ (accessed November 5, 2007).

Gier, H. T. Ecology and Social Behaviour of the Coyote. In M. W. Fox, ed., *The Wild Canids: Their Systematics, Behavioral Ecology and Evolution*. New York: Van Nostrand Reinhold, 1975, 247–262.

Gold, I. K. Effects of Blacktail Prairie Dog Mounds on Shortgrass Vegetation. Unpublished MS thesis, Colorado State University, Fort Collins, 1976.

Graham, R. W., and J. I. Mead. Environmental Fluctuations and Evolution of Mammalian Faunas during the Last Deglaciation in North America. In W. F. Ruddiman and H. E. Wright, eds., *North America and Adja-*

cent Oceans during the Last Deglaciation. Boulder: Geological Society of America, 1987, 371–402.

Himes, D. P. Behavior in an Incipient Black-Tailed Prairie Dog Town. Unpublished MS thesis, Colorado State University, Fort Collins, 1966.

Hoogland, J. L. *The Black-Tailed Prairie Dog: Social Life of a Burrowing Mammal.* Chicago: University of Chicago Press, 1995.

——— (ed.). *Conservation of the Black-Tailed Prairie Dog: Saving North America's Western Grasslands.* Washington, D.C.: Island Press, 2006.

Hoover, J. P. Food Habits of Pronghorn Antelope on Pawnee National Grasslands. Unpublished MS thesis, Colorado State University, Fort Collins, 1971.

Horn, S. W. Mother-Pup Interactions in Coyotes (*Canis latrans*). Unpublished PhD dissertation, Colorado State University, Fort Collins, 1979.

Johnsgard, P. A. *Prairie Dog Empire: A Saga of the Shortgrass Prairie.* Lincoln: University of Nebraska Press, 2005.

Klatt, L. E. A Comparison of the Ecology of Active and Abandoned Black-Tailed Prairie Dog (*Cynomys ludovicianus*) Towns. Unpublished MS thesis, Colorado State University, Fort Collins, 1971.

Lindsey, S. L. The Effect of Food Availability on the Social Organization and Behavior of Captive Coyotes (*Canis latrans*). Unpublished PhD dissertation, Colorado State University, Fort Collins, 1987.

Lundelius, E. L., R. W. Graham, E. Anderson, J. Guilday, J. A. Holman, D. W. Steadman, and S. D. Webb. Terrestrial Vertebrate Faunas. In S. C. Porter, ed., *Late-Quaternary Environments of the United States,* vol. 1, *The Late Pleistocene.* Minneapolis: University of Minnesota Press, 1983, 130–144.

Maxwell, M. H., and L. N. Brown. Ecological Distribution of Rodents on the High Plains of Eastern Wyoming. *Southwestern Naturalist* 13 (1968): 143–158.

Miller, B. J., R. P. Reading, D. E. Biggins, J. K. Detling, S. C. Forrest, J. L. Hoogland, J. Javersak, S. D. Miller, J. Proctor, J. Truett, and D. W. Uresk. Prairie Dogs: An Ecological Review and Current Biopolitics. *Journal of Wildlife Management* 71, no. 8 (2007): 2801–2810.

Myers, G. T., and T. A. Vaughan. Food Habits of the Plains Pocket Gopher in Eastern Colorado. *Journal of Mammalogy* 45 (1964): 588–598.

Powell, E. M. Ecology and Physiology of Free-Ranging Black-Tailed and Utah Prairie Dogs. Unpublished PhD dissertation, Colorado State University, Fort Collins, 2004.

Roach, J. L. Genetic Analysis of a Black-Tailed Prairie Dog (*Cynomys ludovicianus*) Metapopulation within Shortgrass Steppe. Unpublished MS thesis, Colorado State University, Fort Collins, 1999.

Royo, A. R. *Mountain Lion: Felis Concolor.* 1996. http://www.desertusa.com/may96/du_mlion (accessed April 26, 2007).

———. *Mule Deer*. 1997. http://www.desertusa.com/feb97/du_muledeer, (accessed April 26, 2007).

———. *The Pronghorn: Antilocapra americana*. 1999. http://www.desertusa. com/mag99/may/papr/pronghorn (accessed April 26, 2007).

Salmon, T. P., and W. P. Gorenzel. *Voles (Meadow Mice)*. University of California DANR Publication 7439, 2000. http://www.ipm.ucdavis.edu/ PMG/PESTNOTES/ (accessed March 3, 2007).

Savage, C. *Prairie: A Natural History*. Vancouver, B.C.: Greystone Books, 2004.

Savage, L. T. Population Genetics, Fragmentation and Plague in Black-Tailed Prairie Dogs (*Cynomys ludovicianus*). Unpublished PhD dissertation, Colorado State University, Fort Collins, 2007.

Scott, J. R. Behavior and Population Dynamics in a Small Prairie Dog Colony. Unpublished MS thesis, Colorado State University, Fort Collins, 1968.

Semken, H. A. Holocene Mammalian Biogeography and Climatic Change in the Eastern and Central United States. In H. E. Wright Jr., ed., *The Holocene*. Minneapolis: University of Minnesota Press, 1983, 182–207.

Severe, D. S. Revegetation of Blacktail Prairie Dog Mounds on Shortgrass Prairie in Colorado. Unpublished MS thesis, Colorado State University, Fort Collins, 1977.

Sheldon, J. W. *Wild Dogs: The Natural History of the Nondomestic Canidae*. San Diego: Academic Press, 1992.

Stapp, P. A Reevaluation of the Role of Prairie Dogs in Great Plains Grasslands. *Conservation Biology* 12 (1998): 1253–1259.

———. Rodent Communities in Active and Inactive Colonies of Black-Tailed Prairie Dogs in Shortgrass Steppe. *Journal of Mammalogy* 88 (2007): 241–249.

Texas Parks and Wildlife. *Black-Tailed Jackrabbit*. Austin: Texas Parks and Wildlife, 2000. http://www.tpwd.state.tx.us/nature/wild/mammals/ rabbit.htm (accessed November 9, 2006).

Thompson, C. M., D. J. Augustine, and D. M. Mayers. Swift Fox Response to Prescribed Fire in Shortgrass Steppe. *Western North American Naturalist* 68 (2008): 251–256.

Tileston, J. V. Comparison of a White-Tailed Prairie Dog Town with a Black-Tailed Prairie Dog Town in North-Central Colorado. Unpublished MS thesis, Colorado State University, Fort Collins, 1961.

Vaughan, T. A. Food Habits of the Northern Pocket Gopher on Shortgrass Prairie. *American Midland Naturalist* 77 (1967): 176–189.

Vetterling, J. M. Endoparasites of the Black-Tailed Prairie Dog of Northern Colorado. Unpublished MS thesis, Colorado State University, Fort Collins, 1962.

Ward, A. L. Mountain Pocket Gopher Food Habits in Colorado. *Journal of Wildlife Management* 24 (1960): 89–92.

Wilke, C. J. *Mephitis mephitis: Striped Skunk*. University of Michigan, 1996. http://animaldiversity.ummz.umich.edu/accounts/mephitis/m._mephitis (accessed November 9, 2006).

Williams, O., and B. A. Finney. Endogone—A Food for Mice. *Journal of Mammalogy* 45 (1964): 265–271.

Williams, T. T. *Finding Beauty in a Broken World*. New York: Pantheon Books, 2008.

WNC Nature Center. *Eastern Cottontail Rabbit*, 1998. http://wildwnc.org/af/easterncottontailrabbit (accessed November 9, 2006).

PLANTS

Aguilera, M. O. Intraspecific Interactions in Blue Grama. Unpublished PhD dissertation, Colorado State University, Fort Collins, 1992.

Aguilera, M. O., and W. K. Lauenroth. Influence of Gap Disturbances and Type of Microsites on Seedling Establishment in *Bouteloua gracilis*. *Journal of Ecology* 83 (1995): 87–97.

Ares, J. Dynamics of the Root System of Blue Grama. *Journal of Range Management* 29 (1976): 208–213.

Ares, J., and J. S. Singh. A Model of the Root Biomass Dynamics of a Short-grass Prairie Dominated by Blue Grama (*Bouteloua gracilis*). *Journal of Applied Ecology* 11 (1974): 727–744.

Bachelet, D. Simulation of Carbon and Nitrogen Distribution in Blue Grama to Represent Various Kinds of Herbivory. Unpublished PhD dissertation, Colorado State University, Fort Collins, 1983.

Betz, D.-E. Dynamics of Exotic Species in the Pawnee National Grassland, CO, USA. Unpublished MS thesis, Colorado State University, Fort Collins, 2001.

Bonham, C. D., and J. S. Hannan. Blue Grama and Buffalograss Patterns in and Near a Prairie Dog Town. *Journal of Range Management* 31 (1978): 63–65.

Bradford, J. B. The Influence of Climate, Soils, and Land-Use on Primary Productivity and Cheatgrass Invasion in Semi-arid Ecosystems. Unpublished PhD dissertation, Colorado State University, Fort Collins, 2004.

Briske, D. D. Adventitious Root Development in Blue Grama Seedlings. Unpublished PhD dissertation, Colorado State University, Fort Collins, 1977.

Briske, D. D., and A. M. Wilson. Temperature Effects on Adventitious Root Development in Blue Grama Seedlings. *Journal of Range Management* 30 (1977): 276–280.

————. Moisture and Temperature Requirements for Adventitious Root Development in Blue Grama Seedlings. *Journal of Range Management* 31 (1978): 174–178.

————. Drought Effects on Adventitious Root Development in Blue Grama Seedlings. *Journal of Range Management* 33 (1980): 323–327.

Carren, C. J. Effects of Seed Weight and Planting Depth on Emergence and Seedling Growth of Blue Grama. Unpublished MS thesis, Colorado State University, Fort Collins, 1983.

Coffin, D. P., and W. K. Lauenroth. The Effects of Disturbance Size and Frequency on a Shortgrass Plant Community. *Ecology* 69 (1988): 1609–1617.

————. Effects of Competition on Spatial Distribution of Roots of Blue Grama. *Journal of Range Management* 44 (1991): 68–71.

Dye, A. J. Carbon Dioxide Exchange of Blue Grama Swards in the Field. Unpublished PhD dissertation, Colorado State University, Fort Collins, 1972.

Dyer, M. I., and U. G. Bokhari. Plant-Animal Interactions: Studies of the Effects of Grasshopper Grazing on Blue Grama Grass. *Ecology* 57 (1976): 762–772.

Fisher, A. G. Seasonal Trends of Root Reserves in Blue Grama and Western Wheatgrass. Unpublished MS thesis, Colorado State University, Fort Collins, 1966.

Gould, F., and R. B. Shaw (eds.). *Grass Systematics,* 2nd ed. College Station: Texas A&M University Press, 1983.

Hyder, D. N., A. C. Everson, and R. E. Bement. Seedling Morphology and Seedling Failures with Blue Grama. *Journal of Range Management* 24 (1971): 287–292.

Invasive Plants: Changing the Landscape of America. Washington, D.C.: Federal Interagency Committee for the Management of Noxious and Exotic Weeds, 1998.

Jaramillo, V. J., and J. K. Detling. Grazing History, Defoliation, and Competition: Effects on Shortgrass Production and Nitrogen Accumulation. *Ecology* 69 (1988): 1599–1608.

Khan, S. M. Nonstructural Carbohydrates and Tolerance of Dehydration in Blue Grama. Unpublished PhD dissertation, Colorado State University, Fort Collins, 1980.

Kotanen, P. M., J. Bergelson, and D. L. Hazlett. Habitats of Native and Exotic Plants in Colorado Shortgrass Steppe: A Comparative Approach. *Canadian Journal of Botany* 76 (1998): 664–672.

Lajeunesse, S. Dalmatian and Yellow Toadflax. In R. L. Sheley and J. K. Petroff, eds., *Biology and Management of Noxious Rangeland Weeds.* Corvallis: Oregon State University Press, 1999, 202–216.

Lajeunesse, S., R. L. Sheley, C. Duncan, and R. Lym. Leafy Spurge. In R. L. Sheley and J. K. Petroff, eds., *Biology and Management of Noxious Rangeland Weeds*. Corvallis: Oregon State University Press, 1999, 249–260.

Lowe, P. N. Nitrogen Availability Effects on Exotic, Invasive Plant Species. Unpublished MS thesis, Colorado State University, Fort Collins, 2000.

Milchunas, D. G., and W. K. Lauenroth. Three-Dimensional Distribution of Plant Biomass in Relation to Grazing and Topography in the Shortgrass Steppe. *Oikos* 55 (1989): 82–86.

Milchunas, D. G., W. K. Lauenroth, and P. L. Chapman. Plant Competition, Abiotic, and Long- and Short-Term Effects of Large Herbivores on Demography of Opportunistic Species in a Semiarid Grassland. *Oecologia* 92 (1992): 520–531.

Milchunas, D. G., W. K. Lauenroth, P. L. Chapman, and M. K. Kazempour. Effects of Grazing, Topography, and Precipitation on the Structure of a Semiarid Grassland. *Vegetatio* 80 (1989): 11–23.

———. Community Attributes along a Perturbation Gradient in a Shortgrass Steppe. *Journal of Vegetation Science* 1 (1990): 375–384.

Miller, M. S. Blue Grama Growth and Development and Soil Microbial Processes in Atrazine-Treated Microcosms. Unpublished PhD dissertation, Colorado State University, Fort Collins, 1990.

Moore, M. *Medicinal Plants of the Mountain West*. Santa Fe: Museum of New Mexico Press, 1979.

Morishita, D W. Canada Thistle. In R. L. Sheley and J. K. Petroff, eds., *Biology and Management of Noxious Rangeland Weeds*. Corvallis: Oregon State University Press, 1999, 162–174.

Nason, D. A. Spikelet Weight, Seedling Water Uptake Selection, and Shoot Weight in Blue Grama (*Bouteloua gracilis*). Unpublished MS thesis, Colorado State University, Fort Collins, 1981.

Olson, B. E. Impacts of Noxious Weeds on Ecologic and Economic Systems. In R. L. Sheley and J. K. Petroff, eds., *Biology and Management of Noxious Rangeland Weeds*. Corvallis: Oregon State University Press, 1999, 4–18.

Pasture and Range Plants. Bartlesville, Okla.: Phillips Petroleum, 1963.

Roohi, R. Seedling Development and Growth Regulation Effect on Adventitious Root Development of Blue Grama. Unpublished PhD dissertation, Colorado State University, Fort Collins, 1989.

Rowe, H. I. Investigations of Bromus Tectorum: Restoration Strategies and Interactions with Arbuscular Mycorrhizal Fungi. Unpublished PhD dissertation, Colorado State University, Fort Collins, 2006.

Savage, C. *Prairie: A Natural History*. Vancouver, B.C.: Greystone Books, 2004.

Sheley, R. L., S. Kedzie-Webb, and B. D. Maxwell. Integrated Weed Management on Rangeland. In R. L. Sheley and J. K. Petroff, eds., *Biology and*

Management of Noxious Rangeland Weeds. Corvallis: Oregon State University Press, 1999, 57–68.

Sheley, R. L., J. K. Petroff, and M. M. Borman. Introduction. In R. L. Sheley and J. K. Petroff, eds., *Biology and Management of Noxious Rangeland Weeds.* Corvallis: Oregon State University Press, 1999, 1–3.

Sims, P. L., R. K. Lang'at, and D. N. Hyder. Developmental Morphology of Blue Grama and Sand Bluestem. *Journal of Range Management* 26 (1973): 340–344.

Skiles, J. W., J. D. Hanson, and W. J. Parton. Simulation of Above- and Belowground Carbon and Nitrogen Dynamics of *Bouteloua gracilis* and *Agropyron smithii.* In W. K. Lauenroth, G. V. Skogerboe, and M. Flug, eds., *Analysis of Ecological Systems: State-of-the-Art in Ecological Modelling.* Amsterdam: Elsevier, 1983, 467–473.

Stanton, N. L., D. Morrison, and W. A. Laycock. The Effect of Phytophagous Nematode Grazing on Blue Grama Die-off. *Journal of Range Management* 37 (1984): 447–450.

Stump, W. L. The Ecology and Biology of Volunteer Rye (*Secale cereale*), Jointed Goatgrass (*Aegilops cylindrical*), and Downy Brome (*Bromus tectorum*). Unpublished PhD dissertation, Colorado State University, Fort Collins, 1997.

Tilford, G. L. *Edible and Medicinal Plants of the West.* Missoula, Mt.: Mountain Press, 1997.

Uresk, D. W. Dynamics of Blue Grama within a Shortgrass Ecosystem. Unpublished PhD dissertation, Colorado State University, Fort Collins, 1971.

Uresk, D. W., and P. L. Sims. Influence of Grazing on Crude Protein Content of Blue Grama. *Journal of Range Management* 28 (1975): 370–371.

Uresk, D. W., P. L. Sims, and D. A. Jameson. Dynamics of Blue Grama within a Shortgrass Ecosystem. *Journal of Range Management* 28 (1975): 105–108.

Van Der Sluijs, D. H., and D. N. Hyder. Growth and Longevity of Blue Grama Seedlings Restricted to Seminar Roots. *Journal of Range Management* 27 (1974): 117–119.

Walmsley, M. R., J. L. Capinera, J. K. Detling, and M. I. Dyer. Growth of Blue Grama and Western Wheatgrass following Grasshopper Defoliation and Mechanical Clipping. *Journal of the Kansas Entomological Society* 60 (1987): 51–57.

Wilson, A. M., and D. D. Briske. Sediment and Adventitious Root Growth of Blue Grama Seedlings on the Central Plains. *Journal of Range Management* 32 (1979): 209–213.

REPTILES AND AMPHIBIANS

Miller, P. H. A Demographic Study of the Chorus Frog, *Pseudacris triseriata*. Unpublished MS thesis, Colorado State University, Fort Collins, 1977.

Short-Horned Lizard. Royal British Columbia Museum, 1999. http://rbcm1. rbcm.gov.bc.ca/end_species/species (accessed October 12, 2006).

Thompson, S. W. *Prairie Rattlesnake*. 2000. http://www.geocities.com/Baja/ Dunes (accessed October 12, 2006).

RIVERS

Dennehy, K. F., D. W. Little, C. M. Tate, S. L. Qi, P. B. McMahon, B. W. Bruce, R. A. Kimbrough, and J. S. Heiny. 1998. *Water Quality in the South Platte River Basin, Colorado, Nebraska, and Wyoming, 1992–95*. U.S. Geological Survey Circular 1167, Washington, D.C., 38 pp.

Nadler, C. T., and S. A. Schumm. Metamorphosis of South Platte and Arkansas Rivers, Eastern Colorado. *Physical Geography* 2 (1981): 95–115.

Williams, G. P. Historical Perspective of the Platte Rivers in Nebraska and Colorado. In *Lowland River and Stream Habitat in Colorado: A Symposium*. Greeley: Colorado Division of Wildlife, 1978, 11–41.

———. *The Case of the Shrinking Channels—The North Platte and Platte Rivers in Nebraska*. Washington, D.C.: U.S. Geological Survey Circular 781, 1978.

SOIL ECOLOGY

Coleman, D. C., and D. A. Crossley. *Fundamentals of Soil Ecology*. San Diego: Academic Press, 1996.

Jenny, H. *The Soil Resource: Origin and Behavior*. New York: Springer-Verlag, Ecological Studies 37, 1980.

Soil Biology Primer. Washington, D.C.: USDA Natural Resources Conservation Service, 1999.

Wood, M. *Environmental Soil Biology*, 2nd ed. London: Blackie Academic and Professional, 1995.

MISCELLANEOUS

Borror, D. J. *Dictionary of Word Roots and Combining Forms*. Mountain View, Calif.: Mayfield, 1988.

Bowerman, A., B. Brown, A. McMahan, and C. Rutledge. *Ecological Risk Assessment of Chemical Contaminants for the Cathy Fromme Prairie Open Space, Ft. Collins, Colorado*. Part I. Fort Collins: Center for Ecological Risk Assessment and Management, 1996.

City of Fort Collins Natural Areas Management Plan. Fort Collins: City of Fort Collins, Colo., 1992.

Evans, H. E. *Pioneer Naturalists.* New York: Henry Holt, 1993.

Johnsgard, P. A. *Prairie Dog Empire: A Saga of the Shortgrass Prairie.* Lincoln: University of Nebraska Press, 2005.

Jones, S. R. *The Last Prairie: A Sandhills Journal.* New York: McGraw-Hill, 2000.

Newman, M. C. *Fundamentals of Ecotoxicology.* Chelsea, Mich.: Sleeping Bear Press, 1998.

Olson, E. National Grasslands Management: A Primer. Unpublished report, Natural Resources Division, Office of the General Counsel, U.S. Department of Agriculture, Washington, D.C., 1997.

Open Space/Natural Areas Management Team. *Cathy Fromme Prairie Site Management Plan.* Fort Collins: City of Fort Collins Natural Resources Department, 1995.

————. *Site Management Plans for Campeau/Reservoir Ridge, Maxwell, Pineridge, and Coyote Ridge Natural Areas.* Fort Collins: City of Fort Collins Natural Resources Department, 1996.

Ross, J., and B. Ross. *Prairie Time: The Leopold Reserve Revisited.* Madison: University of Wisconsin Press, 1998.

Samson, F., and F. Knopf. Prairie Conservation in North America. *Bioscience* 44 (1994): 418–421.

Samson, F. B., F. L. Knopf, C. W. McCarthy, B. R. Noon, W. R. Ostlie, S. M. Rinehart, S. Larson, G. E. Plumb, G. L. Schenbeck, D. N. Svingen, and T. W. Byer. Planning for Population Viability on Northern Great Plains National Grasslands. *Wildlife Society Bulletin* 31 (2003): 986–999.

Savage, C. *Prairie: A Natural History.* Vancouver, B.C.: Greystone Books, 2004.

Ubbelohde, C., M. Benson, and D. A. Smith. *A Colorado History.* Boulder: Pruett, 1988.

GLOSSARY OF COMMON AND SCIENTIFIC NAMES OF ANIMALS AND PLANTS DESCRIBED IN THE TEXT

ANIMALS

American wigeon	*Anas americana*
badger	*Taxidea taxus*
Baird's sparrow	*Ammodramus bairdii*
bald eagle	*Haliaeetus leucocephalus*
barn owl	*Tyto alba*
bison	*Bison bison*
black bear	*Ursus americanus*
black-billed magpie	*Pica pica*
black-footed ferret	*Mustela nigripes*
black-tailed jackrabbit	*Lepus californicus*

continued on next page

black-tailed prairie dog	*Cynomys ludovicianus*
blue-winged teal	*Anas discors*
bobcat	*Felis rufus*
boreal chorus frog	*Pseudacris triseriata*
broad-tailed hummingbird	*Selasphorus platycercus*
brown-headed cowbird	*Molothrus ater*
brownspotted grasshopper	*Psoloessa delicatula*
bufflehead duck	*Bucephala albeola*
bullsnake	*Pituophis melanoleucus*
burrowing owl	*Athene cunicularia hypugaea*
Canada geese	*Branta canadensis*
Cassin's sparrow	*Aimophila cassinii*
cecropia moth	*Hyalophora cecropia*
cinnamon teal	*Anas cyanoptera*
clay-colored sparrow	*Spizella pallida*
comb-footed spider	*Theridiidae*
common nighthawk	*Chordeiles minor*
common sulfur butterfly	*Colias philodice*
cottontail rabbit	*Sylvilagus floridanus*
coyote	*Canis latrans*
crab spiders	*Philodromidae*
cribellate spiders	*Dictynidae*
darkling beetle	*Eleodes* spp.
deer mouse	*Peromyscus maniculatus*
dusky grasshopper	*Encoptolophus costalis*
eastern yellowbelly racer	*Coluber constrictor flaviventris*
ferruginous hawk	*Buteo regalis*
fox squirrel	*Sciurus niger*
funnel-web weaver spider	*Agelenidae*
gadwall	*Anas strepera*
garter snake	*Thamnophis sirtalis*
Gnaphosid spiders	*Gnaphosidae*
golden eagle	*Aquila chrysaetos*
goldeneye duck	*Bucephala clangula*
grasshopper mouse	*Onychomys leucogaster*
grasshopper sparrow	*Ammodramus savannarum*
great blue heron	*Ardea herodias*
great-horned owl	*Bubo virginianus*

continued on next page

green-veined white butterfly	*Pieris napi*
green-winged teal	*Anas carolinensis*
grizzly bear	*Ursus arctos horribilis*
horned lark	*Eremophila alpestris*
house mouse	*Mus musculus*
Io moth	*Automeris io*
jumping spiders	*Salticidae*
kangaroo rat	*Dipodomys ordii*
kestrel	*Falco sparverius*
lark bunting	*Calamospiza melanocorys*
lesser scaup	*Aythya affinis*
lubber grasshopper	*Brachystola magna*
mallard duck	*Anas platyrynchos*
McCown's longspur	*Calcarius mccownii*
meadow vole	*Microtus pennsylvanicus*
merlin	*Falco columbarius*
monarch butterfly	*Danaus plexippus*
mountain lion	*Felis concolor*
mountain plover	*Charadrius montanus*
mourning dove	*Zenaida macoura*
mule deer	*Odocoileus hemionus*
northern harrier	*Circus cyaneus*
northern pintail	*Anas acuta*
northern shoveler	*Anas clypeata*
pallid tiger swallowtail butterfly	*Pieris protodice*
pipevine swallowtail butterfly	*Battus philenor*
pocket gopher	*Geomys bursarius/ Thomomys talpoides*
polyphemus moth	*Antheraea polyphemus*
prairie falcon	*Falco mexicanus*
prairie rattlesnake	*Crotalus viridis*
prairie vole	*Microtus ochrogaster*
pronghorn antelope	*Antilocapra americana*
pronuba moth	*Tegeticula spp.*
raccoon	*Procyon lotor*
red fox	*Vulpes vulpes*
redhead duck	*Aythya americana*
redlegged grasshopper	*Melanoplus femurrubrum*

continued on next page

red-tailed hawk	*Buteo jamaicensis*
red-winged blackbird	*Agelaius phoeniceus*
ring-necked duck	*Aythya collaris*
river otter	*Lontra canadensis*
Rocky Mountain grasshopper	*Melanoplus spretus*
rough-legged hawk	*Buteo lagopus*
sage grouse	*Centrocercus urophasianus*
screech owl	*Megascops kennicottii*
sharp-shinned hawk	*Accipiter striatus*
sheet-web weaver spider	*Agelenidae*
short-horned lizard	*Phrynosoma douglassii*
soldier beetle	*Cantharidae*
spotted sandpiper	*Arctitis macularia*
spring white butterfly	*Pontia sisymbrii*
striped skunk	*Mephitis mephitis*
Swainson's hawk	*Buteo swainsoni*
swift fox	*Vulpes velox*
thirteen-lined ground squirrel	*Spermophilus tridecemlineatus*
tiger beetle	*Coleoptera* spp.
turkey vulture	*Cathartes aura*
two-spotted skipper butterfly	*Euphyes bimacula*
western bluebird	*Sialia mexicana*
western harvester ant	*Pogonomyrmex occidentalis*
western meadowlark	*Sturnella neglecta*
western scrub jay	*Cyanocitta cristata* ??
white grub (May beetle)	*Phyllophaga fimbripes*
whitelined sphinx moth	*Hyles* spp.
white-tailed deer	*Odocoileus virginiana*
wolf	*Canis lupus*
wolf spider	*Lycosidae*
yellow warbler	*Dendroica petechia*

PLANTS

alkaligrass	*Puccinellia airoides*
alkali sacaton	*Sporobolus airoides*
alyssum	*Alyssum parviflorum*
American licorice	*Glycyrrhiza lepidota*
aster	*Aster* spp.
beardtongue	*Penstemon barbatus*
beeplant	*Cleome serrulata*
big bluestem	*Andropogon gerardii*
bladderpod	*Lesquerella montana*
blue flax	*Adenolinum lewisii*
blue grama	*Bouteloua gracilis*
bluegrass	*Poa* spp.
buffalo grass	*Buchloe dactyloides*
cattail	*Typha* spp.
cheat grass	*Bromus tectorum*
Colorado locoweed	*Oxytropis lambertii*
cordgrass	*Spartina pectinata*
cottonwood	*Populus* spp.
Dalmatian toadflax	*Linaria genistifolia dalmatica*
dandelion	*Taraxacum officinale*
death camas	*Zygadenus venenosus*
European bindweed	*Convolvulus arvensis*
evening primrose	*Oenothera brachycarpa*
field milkvetch	*Astragalus agrestis*
field mint	*Mentha arvensis*
flannel mullein	*Verbascum thapsus*
foxtail barley	*Critesion jubatum*
fringed sage	*Artemisia frigida*
indiangrass	*Sorghastrum* spp.
junegrass	*Koeleria macrantha*
larkspur	*Delphinium* spp.
leafy spurge	*Euphorbia esula*
little bluestem	*Schizachyrium scoparium*
lodgepole pine	*Pinus contorta*
mannagrass	*Glyceria striata stricta*
milkweed	*Asclepias* spp.
mountain mahogany	*Cercocarpus montanus*
muhly	*Muhlenbergia* spp.

continued on next page

needle-and-thread	*Hesperostipa comata*
needlegrass	*Achnatherum nelsonii*
Nuttall's violet	*Viola nuttalli*
plains larkspur	*Delphinium geyeri*
ponderosa pine	*Pinus ponderosa*
poppy mallow	*Callirhoe* spp.
prairie coneflower	*Ratibida columnifera*
prairie threeawn	*Aristida oligantha*
prickly pear cactus	*Opuntia polyacantha*
purple threeawn	*Aristida purpurea*
rabbitbrush	*Chrysothamnus* spp.
reed canarygrass	*Phalaroides arundinacea*
ricegrass	*Achnatherum hymenoides*
rose pussytoes	*Antennaria rosea*
Russian olive	*Eleagnus angustifolia*
sagebrush	*Artemisia* spp.
salsify	*Tragopogon dubius major*
saltgrass	*Distichlis stricta*
sand dropseed	*Sporobolus cryptandrus*
sand lily	*Leucocrinum montanum*
sand reedgrass	*Calamovilfa longifolia*
scarlet gilia	*Ipomopsis aggregata*
scarlet globemallow	*Sphaeralcea coccinea*
Siberian elm	*Ulmus pumila*
sideoats grama	*Bouteloua curtipendula*
silky locoweed	*Oxytropis sericea*
switchgrass	*Panicum virgatum*
Thelesperma	*Thelesperma megapotamicum*
tumbleweed	*Salsola* spp.
wallflower	*Erisymum capitatum*
western wheatgrass	*Agropyron smithii*
western yarrow	*Achillea lanulosa*
wild parsley	*Lomatium foenaculaceum*
willow	*Salix* spp.
yucca (soapweed)	*Yucca glauca*

A PARTIAL LIST OF U.S. AND
CANADIAN GRASSLAND PRESERVES

TALLGRASS

Konza Prairie, Kansas (The Nature Conservancy)
Midewin National Tallgrass Prairie, Illinois
Nachusa Grasslands Preserve, Illinois (The Nature Conservancy)
Sheyenne National Grassland, North Dakota
Tallgrass Prairie National Preserve, Kansas

MIXED GRASS

Badlands National Park, South Dakota
Black Kettle National Grassland, Oklahoma and Texas
Buffalo Gap National Grassland, South Dakota

Cedar River National Grassland, North Dakota
Charles M. Russell National Wildlife Refuge, Montana
Cross Ranch Preserve, North Dakota (The Nature Conservancy)
Curlew National Grassland, Idaho
Fort Pierre National Grassland, South Dakota
Grand River National Grassland, North Dakota
Little Missouri National Grassland, North Dakota
McClellan Creek National Grassland, Texas
Niobrara Valley Preserve, Nebraska (The Nature Conservancy)
Ordway Prairie Preserve, North Dakota (The Nature Conservancy)
Wind Cave National Park, South Dakota
Grasslands National Park, Canada

SHORTGRASS

Cimarron National Grassland, Kansas
Comanche National Grassland, Colorado
Kiowa National Grassland, New Mexico
Oglala National Grassland, Nebraska
Pawnee National Grassland, Colorado
Rita Blanca National Grassland, New Mexico
Smith Ranch Preserve, Colorado (The Nature Conservancy)
Soapstone Prairie Natural Area, Colorado
Thunder Basin National Grassland, Wyoming

SAGEBRUSH STEPPE

Crooked River National Grassland, Oregon

INDEX

Ant: western harvester, 102–104, 192, 202, 216

Antelope, pronghorn, 93, 152, 174–75, 176, 215; absence from Fromme Prairie, 47, 126, 174; association with prairie dogs, 126, 132; hunting of, 48, 49; references about, 205

Arapaho people, 50–51, 183

Archaic people, 48

Badger, 30, 46, 121, 136, 157, 178, 213

Beetle: darkling, 93, 106, 115, 214; soldier, 110, 216; tiger, 96, 216

Bindweed, 128, 147, 155, 173, 217

Bird, Isabella, 10–11, 116

Bison, 20, 23, 31, 34, 213; absence from Fromme Prairie, 30, 180; association with prairie dogs, 126, 132; grazing by, 28, 41, 61, 78, 79, 110, 175, 176; historical large numbers of, 3, 9, 32, 49, 50, 117, 124; hunting of, 22, 48, 152, 175, 180

Blackbird, red-winged, 121, 128, 216

Blue grama, 4, 46, 68, 73, 85, 86, 94, 96, 111, 115, 117, 125, 128, 138, 153, 179, 217; adaptations of to drought, 13, 42, 69–70, 72; dormancy of, 183, 186, 190; establishment and growth of, 43, 70–72, 80–81, 83, 89, 103–104, 124; morphology of, 75–77; response and adaptations to grazing, 41, 42, 74–75, 79–80, 100–102; references about, 199, 200, 207, 208, 209, 210. *See also* Grass

Bubonic plague, 123, 133, 206

Buteo jamaicensis. See Hawk: red-tailed

Butterfly: green-veined white, 157, 215; monarch, 108, 157, 215; spring white, 98, 216; swallowtail, 98, 157, 215; two-spotted skipper, 107–108, 203, 216

Bunting, lark, xiii, 45–47, 215

C_3 plants, 13, 42

C_4 plants, 13, 41–42, 69

221

Canis latrans. *See* Coyote

Carbon, 6, 84, 138; and plant metabolism, 13, 80–81, 101; cycling within soil of, 58, 59, 60, 76–78, 80–82, 94, 176; exchange between atmosphere and plants, 12–13, 80–81, 91, 182; references about, 201, 207, 208, 210

Cather, Willa, 12, 24, 183, 192, 195

Cattail, 66, 83, 124, 128, 140, 148, 157, 183, 217

Cattle, 3, 32, 60, 83, 152, 175–76, 177, 181; grazing by, 31, 41, 42, 79, 85, 90, 101, 114, 176; overgrazing by, 123–24; references about, 204. *See also* Cow

Central Plains Experimental Range (CPER), 60, 62; animals of, 43–45, 47, 100, 104, 175, 176; archeology and prehistory of, 48, 49, 50; history of and research at, 40, 51, 59; plants of, 41–43

Cheat grass, 34, 40, 172, 217; at the CPER, 41–43; at the Fromme Prairie, 87–88, 90, 127; references about, 207

Cheyenne people, 50–51

Clovis people, 21, 47

Colorado Front Range, 52, 65, 167, 172, 181, 199

Comanche National Grassland, 33, 40, 47, 220

Comanche people, 49–50, 196

Cottonwood, 2, 86, 158, 170, 183, 187–88, 217; human uses of, 148–49

Cow. *See* Cattle

Cowbird, brown-headed, 108, 110, 172, 183, 214

Coyote, 1, 4, 5, 20, 67, 93, 147, 148, 149, 150, 153, 155, 158–59, 160, 161, 179, 183, 188, 214; behavior and physiology of, 141–42, 144–45, 148, 151–52; growth and rearing of young, 73, 141–42, 144, 152, 154–55, 157, 159; human killing of, 48, 151; hunting by, 46, 47, 99, 132, 136, 138–39, 141–43, 147, 186; references about, 204, 205, 212

Cretaceous Interior Seaway, 10, 16, 84

Cynomys ludovicianus. *See* Prairie dog

Dalmatian toadflax, 87–88, 208, 217

Death camas, 73, 217

Deer, mule, 57, 78, 152, 159, 186, 188, 215; behavior of, 174, 175; references about, 206

Denver, Colorado, 25, 50–51

Dove, mourning, 107, 153, 215

Drought, 20, 61, 128; historical occurrences of, 26, 31, 58, 85, 123; plant adaptations to, 13, 26, 28, 41, 42, 43, 70, 72, 74, 79, 80, 82; references about, 208

Duck: black-headed scaup, 73; gadwall, 149–50, 214; lesser scaup, 149, 215; mallard, 61, 149, 215; northern shoveler, 149, 215; redhead, 73, 149, 215; ring-necked, 149, 216

Dung, 82–83

Dust Bowl, 26, 40, 58, 85

Eagle: bald, 2, 73, 188, 213; golden, 61, 67, 130–32, 151, 157, 170–71, 214

Earthworm, 61, 67, 91, 93, 179; predation on, 158, 171, 177; references about, 203; and soil ecology, 75, 78–80, 94, 137

El Niño, 25, 31

Exotic plants, 34, 39–43, 61–62, 90, 132, 156, 172, 207–209. *See also* Invasive plants

Falcon, prairie, 67, 107, 132, 170, 215

Ferret, black-footed, 33, 132, 213

Fire, 34, 45, 49, 85; historical accounts of, 9, 25, 27; and prairie vegetation, 27–28, 30, 41, 61, 70, 79, 88, 128, 172, 175; references about, 200, 201, 202, 204, 206

Folsom people, 47–48

Fort Collins, Colorado, 2–3, 45, 51, 147, 182

Fossil Creek, 66, 86, 137, 141, 145, 148, 167, 170, 174

Fox: red, 39, 47, 61, 73, 93, 136, 141, 143–44, 155, 159, 188, 215; swift, 33, 46, 47, 132, 136, 206, 216

Frémont, John Charles, 50, 121–22, 148, 192–93, 196–97

Frog: boreal chorus, 73, 93, 214

Fur trapping, 50, 151

Geese: Canada, 73, 189, 214

Grass: alkaligrass, 73, 217; big bluestem, 43, 67, 156, 217; blue grama, 4, 13, 41–43, 46, 68–81, 83, 85–86, 89, 93–94, 96, 100–104, 111, 115, 117, 124–25, 128, 138, 153, 179, 183, 186–87, 190, 199–200, 207–210, 217; bluegrass, 73, 147, 217; buffalograss, 20, 74, 86, 94, 96, 185, 207, 217; bunch, 41, 67, 74–77, 96–98, 105, 111, 125, 145, 147; cordgrass, 73, 127, 217; dropseed, 13, 73, 218; foxtail barley, 173, 217; indiangrass, 73, 217; junegrass,